CLOSING THE INNOVATION GAP

CLOSING THE INNOVATION GAP

REIGNITING THE SPARK OF CREATIVITY IN A GLOBAL ECONOMY

JUDY ESTRIN

New York   Chicago   San Francisco   Lisbon
London   Madrid   Mexico City   Milan   New Delhi
San Juan   Seoul   Singapore   Sydney   Toronto

1 2 3 4 5 6 7 8 9 0   DOC/DOC   0 9 8

ISBN: 978-0-07-149987-3
MHID: 0-07-149987-3

Illustrations by Susan Kare.

This publication is designed to provide accurate and authoritative information in regard to the subject matter covered. It is sold with the understanding that the publisher is not engaged in rendering legal, accounting, or other professional service. If legal advice or other expert assistance is required, the services of a competent professional person should be sought.
>   —*From a declaration of principles jointly adopted by a committee of the*
>   *American Bar Association and a committee of publishers.*

McGraw-Hill books are available at special quantity discounts to use as premiums and sales promotions, or for use in corporate training programs. To contact a representative please visit the Contact Us pages at www.mhprofessional.com.

Library of Congress Cataloging-in-Publication Data

Estrin, Judy.
  Closing the innovation gap : reigniting the spark of creativity
in a global economy / by Judy Estrin.
     p. cm.
  Includes bibliographical references and index.
  ISBN 0-07-149987-3 (alk. paper)
  1. Technological innovations—Management. 2. New products.
3. Entrepreneurship. I. Title.

HD45.E74 2009
658.4'063—dc22   2008011676

This book is dedicated to future innovators
all over the world.

CONTENTS

PREFACE

My teenage son, David, is an innovator—not just in his creative writing or his music, but also in his approach to life. Never afraid to ask questions, he balances risk taking with good judgment, combines tenacity with self-confidence, and pushes the limits of whatever he is working on. He is an avid user of technology for schoolwork, communicating with friends, and pursuing his passions of poetry, photography, music, and filmmaking. But he is not likely to grow up to be a scientist.

As he started high school and we began to talk about college, David went online to explore careers that might catch his interest. I started thinking about why so few of his friends seem interested in science, and what life will be like for him and his children when they enter the workplace. I began to think more broadly about innovation. What had inspired my generation's broad interest in science? What's different now? The last decade has brought about so much change in science, in business, and in our country.

My life and my career benefited from an environment in which scientific and technological innovation and entrepreneurialism were at their best. My parents were professors and pioneers in the development and application of computer technology. My father, Gerald Estrin, was one of the founders of UCLA's computer science department. My mother, Thelma Estrin, got her Ph.D. in electrical engineering in 1951, when only one other woman in the country earned such a degree. She went on to a career in biomedical engineering and served as a director at the National Science Foundation (NSF) for two years in the early 1980s. My childhood was steeped in science to such an extent that it never occurred to me or to my siblings that we would choose any other path. My older sister, Margo, is a doctor of internal medicine, and my younger sister, Deborah, is a professor of computer science. Both are innovators in their respective fields.

When I enrolled at UCLA in 1971, the first seeds of what would become the Internet were just starting to sprout at universities and research labs funded by the Department of Defense. After witnessing the excitement of these pioneering attempts to link computers in different parts of the globe, I wanted to be part of the action, and I moved north to do graduate work at Stanford University, located in the heart of what we now call Silicon Valley. I was the youngest and only female member of a research team led by Vint Cerf, a computer science pioneer who would later be called the father of the Internet. Cerf's team of graduate students was developing a new kind of networking software—the code that allows computers to exchange information—called Transmission Control Protocol, or TCP. We all felt that we were working on something important. Little did we know, however, that the software we were developing would become the cornerstone of the Internet and the World Wide Web.

Then serendipity happened, and I was ready. My first job was at a computing start-up called Zilog, where I discovered the magic of working as part of a small, talented team. I also realized that my real passion and skill were not for interacting with machines, but for working with people to bring new technology to market. Surprising everyone in my family, including myself, I evolved into a business leader and entrepreneur. I met my former husband, Bill Carrico, at Zilog. When we started a networking company called Bridge Communications in 1981, we never imagined that we would end up launching seven companies together. My career was spent primarily working on the "plumbing" of the Internet, developing products that most people weren't even aware of unless a problem came up. Then Cisco Systems acquired our third venture, Precept Software, in 1998, and I found myself in the role of chief technology officer for one of the fastest-growing companies in history.

I have also had the opportunity to work with the leaders of several large companies for which a consistent flow of innovative ideas has provided a critical competitive advantage. I joined the board of FedEx in 1989, of Rockwell in 1994, of Sun Microsystems in 1995, and of The Walt Disney Company in 1998. I continue to serve the shareholders of both FedEx and Disney today. Many of the stories in this book have been drawn from my experiences and contacts in these companies. I think of FedEx and Disney as two complementary hemispheres of the "mind" of innovation. FedEx is driven by operational excellence—the ultimate left-brain company. At the heart of Disney are creativity and imagination, embodying the indispensable aptitudes of the right brain. Both companies are well managed, customer focused, strategic, and visionary. And both have benefited the lives of millions of people by staying true to their commitment to the future.

At the peak of the Internet bubble in 2000, I left Cisco with a growing concern about the state of innovation in the technology industry. Silicon Valley had changed. The excitement of solving interesting problems by creating new technology was fading, and immediate financial returns were taking precedence over the mission of building lasting companies. I wanted to return to running my own company, but I didn't want to start a product-centered business that would be pushed into the short-term, frenetic mode that had swept the industry. So with our next venture, Packet Design, we experimented with a different model—a perpetual start-up that would explore future technologies, nurture new ideas, and spin out separate companies to take products to market.

The two years following my fiftieth birthday in 2004 were full of transitions. Bill Carrico and I decided to go our separate ways after being marriage and business partners for 25 years. Following the collapse of the dot-com bubble, Packet Design stopped funding new projects. I knew it was time for something new both inside and out. Looking forward to the next phase of my life, I found myself experiencing both the anticipation and the anxiety of having virtually unconstrained freedom to choose my next step. Innovation starts with a capacity for change. What did I want to do?

I was fortunate to be born at a time when the nation understood the importance of science, technology, and innovation, and encouraged taking risks. Along with many other scientists, businesspeople, and parents, I'm convinced that my son's generation will not have the same opportunities that I enjoyed, as the country has become increasingly more focused on short-term gains. This book was born from my need to try to do something about this shift by sharing my perspectives.

To reclaim our stake in the future, we will need to think broadly, be bold, and take responsibility for the problems that we've created. While appreciating the strategies for sustainable innovation that worked in the past, we also need to adapt to today's new economic and social realities. Many groups need to be involved in solving this problem, including businesses, government organizations, financial institutions, nonprofits, academics, educators, and parents. To move forward effectively, this diverse set of players will require a common framework and language.

One of my first lessons in effective problem solving came from my father. When I was a student at UCLA, there were no personal computers; everyone shared time on big mainframes, submitting programs and getting the results back hours later. I remember staying up all night for my first programming class, nearly in tears because each time my printouts came back, the word ABEND (short for "abnormal ending") glared at me. My program had crashed. When I would come home overwhelmed, my father would remind me to try to break the problem into smaller, more solvable pieces, while keeping in mind how they all fit together. That is the approach that I have taken to the problem of innovation.

Closing the Innovation Gap draws on my experiences as well as on interviews with more than 100 scientists, engineers, entrepreneurs, venture capitalists, researchers, educators, and academic and business leaders who have been contributors to America's innovative excellence. The first two chapters present a framework for understanding the process of sustainable innovation, including the concept of an Innovation Ecosystem, and the five core values that give individuals, businesses, organizations, and nations the capacity for change. In Chapters 3 through 5, I review the evolution of science and technology in the decades since World War II, identifying what worked well and what went wrong. I conclude with a perspective on key issues that will need to be addressed in order to reignite broad innovation. Chapter 6 illustrates the application of the innovation framework at an organizational level. Chapters 7 and 8 focus on the national Innovation Ecosystem and what can be done to ensure its enduring health.

For the sake of David's generation and those that will follow, I hope this book will provide a fresh perspective, provoking others to consider the consequences of their decisions on innovation—for themselves personally and for their organizations, their countries, and the world.

CLOSING
THE
INNOVATION
GAP

INTRODUCTION

INNOVATION
IS NOT OPTIONAL

Innovation, exploration, freedom, and renewal—these ideals have sustained the vitality of American culture and business since the pilgrims sailed west and the founding fathers launched an ambitious new kind of democracy. For three centuries, our national identity was synonymous with bold risk taking and historical firsts: the pioneering expeditions to the North and South Poles, the earliest self-powered airplane flight, and the brave first steps on the moon.

Leading-edge science and technology have been the foundation of our country's economic growth. Our strength in bringing new ideas to market has enabled us to trade and compete effectively with other nations, improving the lives of people all over the world. "In short, if Americans stop innovating," declared the National Council on Competitiveness in 2005, "we stop being Americans."

Today, more than ever, innovation is critical to the role we will play in the global economy. But do we still have what it takes to succeed? Great companies often fail when they take their success for granted. And so, too, can great societies. There are ever-increasing signs that we should be concerned about our future. The United States, along with the rest of the world, faces major challenges—dependence on oil, climate change, health care, and national security—that threaten our economy and our quality

1

of life. Each of these challenges also brings opportunities—*if* we give innovation the attention it deserves.

To face these all-important issues from a position of strength, businesses and the nation's leadership must think beyond short-term financial results and understand the impact of globalization and an accelerated pace of change on future economic growth. Those companies that embrace these challenges, viewing them as opportunities to develop new products, lower their costs, or improve their reputations, will benefit over the long term.

Scientific innovation is not important only to scientists and to the U.S. economy. It affects everyone. When I was chief technology officer at Cisco Systems, I began each presentation by saying, "The Internet is changing the way we work, live, learn, and play." The World Wide Web is only one example of technological innovation that has had a profound impact on all of us.

New medical procedures, genetic testing, and scientific evidence about how lifestyle affects wellness influence how long we live. Medication is now available to help us maintain and optimize our physical, mental, and sexual health. Breakthroughs in battery technology have enabled new portable devices that free us from being chained to our desks, giving workers and executives new levels of mobility and flexibility. Cell phones, e-mail, and instant messaging have transformed the ways we interact. New devices and technologies such as iPods, TiVo, IPTV, and low-cost digital video cameras allow consumers to choose when and how they want to be entertained. User-created content and social networking Web sites like Facebook are increasing the speed and influence of word of mouth and putting more power in the hands of the consumer.

The once-groundbreaking products that now seem commonplace—such as nonstick cookware, the GPS systems in cars, and prescription drugs that control high blood pressure—were not developed in a vacuum. They were all built on a strong and deep foundation of research, development, and application of science and technology going back years or even decades. I call this continuum the Innovation Ecosystem.

INNOVATION IS NOT JUST A SOUND BITE

Is innovation magic, a stroke of luck, or just another process that needs to be managed? Are innovators born or taught? Is it enough to mandate an innovative culture, or does it also need to be nurtured? Whether you're involved in innovation for a company, an agency, a charity, or yourself, or indirectly influencing innovation through policy or education, it's important to understand what really drives productive change.

In searching for the best way to describe how innovation can be encouraged and nurtured, I thought back to my early science education. It was so exciting to see a tide pool for the first time. The many inhabitants of that small square of water, each with its own defense system against the hazards of the changing tides—sea anemones, crabs, mussels, and more—coexisted for their mutual benefit. Biological ecosystems that sustain life are models for the organizations, people, and forces that enable innovation. Life flourishes because of a dynamic interaction between communities of living organisms and their environment. As you look deeper into these ecosystems, you learn that different types of organisms—each with its own distinctive life cycle—are cooperating and collaborating to ensure the vitality of the whole system. Well-understood, orderly phenomena exist side by side with seemingly more random ones. Many of these phenomena also apply to innovation.

In Innovation Ecosystems, the collaborative organisms include scientists, product developers, businesspeople, service providers, and customers, all of whom participate in one or more of three communities: *research, development,* and *application*. Ongoing, sustainable innovation results from interactions between these communities at an organizational, national, and global level.

A beautiful flower or a luscious bunch of grapes begins with seeds. The right combination of soil, water, and air determines how well it grows. For innovation to thrive, the environment must also be right. Leadership style, adequate funding, and policy must all be aligned to fuel the innovation process. Education and culture also play indispensable roles by training, inspiring, and motivating the innovators of the future.

Just as there are basic laws that underlie biological ecosystems, there is a set of core values that must work in balance to support innovation: *questioning, risk taking, openness, patience,* and *trust*. These values are the foundation of innovation. As a group, they determine the *capacity for change* of an individual, organization, or nation.

Each biological ecosystem has its own unique elements, maintaining a delicate balance that sustains life. Without this balance in our Innovation Ecosystems, we risk the possibility that we will be unable to create the new discoveries, products, and ideas that will be required for our success.

Given the number of innovative products and services that we see around us, it's easy to believe that our Ecosystem is stable and secure. But in fact, we are rapidly losing our advantage. Innovation is not just a sound bite, and a focus on the short term is not enough. Both our companies and the country have dangerous blind spots in the areas of medium-term and long-term innovation. We're all a bit like characters in the Road Runner cartoons: running off the cliff and hanging in midair with grins on our faces, not yet realizing that the once-solid ground below us is no longer there. But we cannot simply retreat to the cliff by clinging to what worked in the last century. We must understand the fundamentals of innovation, learn from our past successes and failures, and identify the forces that shifted the balance in favor of near-term results. As we look forward to a paradigm for the twenty-first century, we need to account for how much has changed.

The Internet took more than 30 years to go from research to ubiquity. Our ability to initiate and sustain levels of innovation that will further transform the world, as the World Wide Web has done, will be crucial to securing a safe, productive, and creative future. Ironically, as the global economy we helped create has become increasingly interconnected and competitive, America has lost the core values that were the catalysts of its success. We can—and must—regain our momentum, adapt to a new reality, and restore our culture of innovation and commitment to science at all levels of society. If we do not, we will lose our position of strength, and with it our hopes for ongoing economic prosperity and enhanced quality of life for our children and grandchildren.

INNOVATION PROCESS

Talent

CORE VALUES

- **?** QUESTIONING
- 🕐 PATIENCE
- ⚓ TRUST
- 👁 OPENNESS
- 🎲 RISK

CHAPTER 1

THE CAPACITY FOR CHANGE

Say the word *Pixar* and what comes to mind? Kids of all ages think of *Toy Story, A Bug's Life, Monsters Inc, Finding Nemo, The Incredibles, Cars,* and *Ratatouille.* All of these films create magical worlds in which toys, bugs, monsters, fish, superheroes, and cars come to life, and a rat can become a gourmet chef. Even after my son was too old to want to go to the theater with me, I eagerly awaited the release of each new Pixar film—not only to watch what great story would unfold, but also to see how the company's brilliant animators pushed technology to make their onscreen characters even more engaging. At Pixar, the technology inspires the art and the art challenges the technology. It's a two-way street.

I remember my first visit to Pixar headquarters in Emeryville, California, when Disney was in the process of acquiring the company. The lobby opens into a giant atrium surrounded by conference rooms, gaming spaces, and a cafeteria, inviting employees to play, meet, eat, and create. Scooters and skateboards are used to zip around the building, encouraging people to get out of their offices and move around. The openness of the building immediately conveys the openness of the environment.

Walking through the door of the animation department is like entering a Pixar movie—or a bustling small town. The workspace is decorated thematically for each new film. On the day I visited, there were rats everywhere (cute ones, of course) because the project in production was *Ratatouille*. Each animator creates his or her own unique workspace. One had built a little cottage out of a gardening shed; another, who prefers to work standing up, designed an office with no walls and no chairs. It was clear how much thought had been put into creating a physical environment that inspires individualism, creativity, and fun.

Behind Pixar's incredible creative and financial success is leadership that has a deep understanding of the importance and process of innovation. Launched with $10 million by Ed Catmull and John Lasseter in 1986, the company was sold to Disney for over $7 billion in 2006. Catmull is now the president of Disney and Pixar Animation Studios. Lasseter, who is the chief creative officer, is often referred to as the next Walt Disney.

The genesis of the company was an example of innovation at work. What is now Pixar began in 1979 when George Lucas, of *Star Wars* fame, set up a group to explore new techniques for digital printing and audio and video editing. He hired Catmull, a leading researcher in computer graphics, who has always had a passion for filmmaking. After several years, they agreed to set up the group as an independent company. Following months of discussions with venture capitalists (VCs) and corporate partners that led nowhere, they finally negotiated a deal with Apple founder Steve Jobs, who was attracted by the talent of the team. Their passion was to make full-length computer-generated animated films. But recognizing that neither the technology nor the market was ready, they sold advanced imaging systems to medical-imaging firms, government agencies, and other movie studios, including Disney. Never giving up on their long-term vision, a small group led by Lasseter developed animated short films that helped drive the technologists and incubated what would eventually become Pixar's main business.

From 1986 to 1991, Pixar went through several variations of its business strategy. "We were grasping for a workable model. We sold the hardware business and started to sell software. Then we started making TV commercials," Catmull recalls. "Throughout, we struggled. Steve stuck with us as we were losing money. Then Disney gave us the opportunity to do a feature film."

If the team had been less passionate and tenacious, there would be no *Toy Story* or *Cars*. If the company had been backed by typical venture capitalists instead of a visionary entrepreneur like Jobs, it would never have survived its various transitions. Although he is not usually thought of as a patient personality, Jobs provided patient capital for the company. He trusted the smart people on the team, recognizing that their attempts to create various business models were not fatal failures, but steps toward success. When Disney approached Pixar in 1991 to work together on a set of 3D computer-animated feature films, the company and its technology were ready.

How has the company managed to always stay out ahead of the competition, each film amazing audiences more than the one before? Part of the answer is that the technology organization is always working on three time horizons simultaneously. Pixar developers who are dedicated to the next film in the lineup work side by side with the directors, writers, and animators to apply and extend the current technology. Other developers work on the next generation of animation tools so that the characters and environments in future films are even more real—enabling water to flow, shiny cars to reflect light, and fur to look soft to the touch. Pixar also has a small applied research group that focuses on longer-term development. This group collaborates with the research community at large on new algorithms that continually push the state of the art of graphics and animation.

Pixar's internal culture encourages creativity through questioning, openness, and a healthy attitude toward failure. Self-assessment is ongoing—not only when there's a problem, but also when things seem to be working well. Everyone is encouraged to comment on one another's work. "We have a group of filmmakers who don't take critiques personally. Here, it would be a serious error not to say what you thought," says Catmull. This level of honesty requires a working environment in which people trust management and feel safe.

Employees are encouraged to make their ideas available for feedback early. "People not only have to be willing to take risks, but others have to be willing to let them take the risk," Catmull observes. "Our first job is to get to the failure as soon as possible." Then they figure out why they failed and fix the things they couldn't foresee. Instead of viewing failures as negative, they recognize the initial missteps as necessary to getting the feedback needed to develop an important software tool or a brilliant film.

Pixar produces great entertainment by employing the best talent in research, development, and application of technology. The company has a shared vision and an unwavering commitment to the core values and process of innovation.

THE BASIC INGREDIENTS

Sustainable innovation does not happen in a vacuum. It is not just a flash of brilliance from a lone scientist, nor is it simply the result of a group going offsite to brainstorm and play team-building games. People often overestimate the *aha!* factor in the invention process. That process starts with creating the right kind of environment. "The rare thing is not coming up with ideas. It is creating that soup where lots of people are coming up with ideas, and having a system that translates them into something effective," says Danny Hillis, a former Disney Imagineer and cofounder of Applied Minds, an R&D consulting firm that calls itself the "little Big Idea company." The soup starts with some common ingredients, a set of human attitudes and beliefs that are so critical that I call them the five core values of innovation: *questioning, risk taking, openness, patience,* and *trust.*

If pushed to an extreme, any one of these values can actually stifle innovation. Trust without questioning is blind. Too much patience can create an environment in which nothing happens. Risk taking must be tempered by questioning so that it does not become reckless. Questioning without trust can become merely judgmental. When all five values are in balance, they work together to create the capacity for change that enables innovation to thrive.

Questioning

Innovators naturally ask why or how something works, or if something can be done in a new way. This curiosity is encouraged by giving them room to explore. "My folks would be at home working on technology whether I paid them or not," says Miley Ainsworth, IT director for FedEx Labs. "They have a natural hunger for new stuff. Technology happens to be their job, but it's also their hobby." Author and consultant John Seely Brown, former chief scientist at Xerox, calls himself "Chief of Confusion, helping people ask the right questions." This restless curiosity inspires innovators to uncover promise and potential that others have overlooked.

In the early days of the ARPANET—the predecessor of the Internet—the focus of development was on creating networks that would allow computers in disparate geographical locations to communicate. But Bob Metcalfe, then at Xerox, became curious about the data being exchanged between computers in the same building, which had been nicknamed "incestuous traffic." Out of this curiosity came the development of Ethernet, the foundation of local area networks that enable individuals to share information with their coworkers, friends, and family.

David Culler, a computer science professor at UC Berkeley, describes this kind of inquisitiveness as "stubbing my toe on the same spot often enough that I say, 'What is this?' Then I look down and find that what I'm tripping on is just the tip of a very big rock below the surface." Innovation can also be driven by curiosity about things that *don't* exist. "Once, when my three-year-old son was learning to read road signs," says Culler, "he asked me, 'Dad, why aren't there any "go" signs?' Kids see these things. What else are we not seeing?"

The only way to get beyond mere incremental improvements is to question the status quo. When Tesla Motors introduced its flashy red electric sports car in 2006, it made a big splash. People lined up to place orders for a car that hadn't even been built yet. The Tesla was not the first electric car to hit the market, but its reception was different because the company's cofounder, Martin Eberhard, was willing to take a new approach. All of the prior efforts to market electric cars had prioritized affordability to reach the broadest possible market. "They made horrible little cars that nobody wanted to drive," says Eberhard. Instead, Tesla decided to launch with a high-end model that was outright cool to create desirability for the product concept; later it would figure out how to make a more affordable version. Whether the company is successful over the long term or not, Eberhard's willingness to buck the trend has created positive, disruptive changes in the electric-car industry.

Entrepreneur Randy Scott launched a start-up called Incyte to sequence and catalog genes with the goal of discovering new drugs. But the genetic data themselves turned out to be Incyte's most valuable asset. "We created one of the first information-based business models in biotech to generate gene-sequence information and sell it to big pharmaceutical companies," says Scott. He feared that Incyte would end up in a mad race with dozens of other companies jumping into the emerging biotech market. But because of its unique business model, Incyte had few competitors. "Everyone was caught up in the idea that the only way to make money in biotech was to develop a new drug. The idea of selling the information was just too different," Scott recalls. Eventually, the company grew to over $200 million a year in sales because its founders were willing to adopt a new way of doing business.

Scott's next venture grew out of a more personal kind of questioning—asking why there were so few effective medical interventions available to a good friend who was diagnosed with breast cancer. His friend's treatment plan included chemotherapy, which had a remote chance of putting her cancer into remission, but would surely make her gravely ill. "I asked myself why we weren't using all the information we could get out of the genome to classify tumors better," says Scott. Leveraging the growing global bank of genetic data, he launched a company called Genomic Health to provide more personalized medicine, identifying treatments targeted to the genetic makeup of an individual patient and his or her specific disease. In the end, it was too late for Scott to help his friend, but not to bring the benefits of genomically targeted medicine to millions of others.

The way that leaders ask questions affects motivation and behavior, setting the tone for the whole organization. Questions can be inquisitive or judgmental. They can convey interest or impatience. Asking, "Why did you . . .?" conveys judgment, not trust. Similar information can be gleaned by asking, "Can you explain . . . ?" The types of questions that are critical to managing an ongoing project—"When will this be done? What are the milestones to measure progress or success?"—can also suppress new ideas. Research projects often consist of a set of open-ended questions or hypotheses that are being investigated without a clear outcome or end date. That doesn't mean that you shouldn't ask *what* the researchers are working on and *how* they plan to move forward. Leaders also need to be open to being questioned by others and themselves.

As we mature, we're more prone to take situations as givens and forget to question the status quo or ourselves. With more to lose, we may be less willing to take risks. The same thing can happen as companies, industries, and fields of science mature and innovation becomes more incremental. But just as midlife can be viewed as a time of positive change, mature companies, industries, and scientists should continue to question their assumptions and pursue bold, broad-ranging innovation. Change may be more difficult at that stage, but curiosity and assessment should not stop with age or growth.

Risk

Accepting failure is not easy, and it is often costly in terms of dollars and reputation. It's hard for people to give up when they passionately believe in a vision. But tolerance and patience are necessary if you want people to take creative and promising risks. FedEx CIO Rob Carter credits part of his company's success to having a healthy attitude toward failure. "Failure is painful, and we struggle with it," he admits. "But we have a great culture around bold risk taking."

Failure is an inherent part of innovation. "When you start a project, you don't know enough about the competition or the customer needs. You haven't developed the best ideas or the best technology," says Curtis Carlson, CEO of SRI International, an independent nonprofit R&D organization. "So it's the nature of the game that in the beginning, most of what you're going to do is going to be a failure."

People need to trust that they will not be labeled as career flops if they have done their jobs well and understand why their ideas or projects did not succeed. Failures should not be personalized unless they result from poor execution or lack of effort. Aim for accountability without finger-pointing and blame.

FedEx acquired a transportation company called Flying Tigers in 1989 as part of the company's international expansion strategy. "We were very aggressive in Europe in the late 1980s and early 1990s, and got ahead of ourselves," admits CEO Fred Smith. "We had to restructure those businesses, but we treated everyone fairly. You have to recognize that some things won't work out. Then you've got to regroup and not shoot the people who made a valiant effort." Instead, FedEx built out its Express Freighter network and narrowed its focus in Europe, which has become the company's most profitable international market. By buying Flying Tigers, the company also acquired landing rights in Asia that are critical to its business worldwide.

The loss of more than a billion dollars through the purchase and subsequent sale of a company called Musicland taught Best Buy a significant enough lesson to catalyze a complete rethinking of its leadership construct. "The acquisition made sense to people at the top," says Kal Patel, Best Buy's enthusiastic executive VP, who spends his time in Asia and Silicon Valley searching for innovative people and ideas. But while the company's executives were busy spinning out a rationale for buying a retail music company, Napster burst onto the Net and changed all the rules. Suddenly millions of teenagers decided that music should be downloadable—and free. "That was a pivotal moment for us," Patel recalls. "We became much more focused on recognizing and fulfilling both articulated and unarticulated consumer needs." Best Buy launched an internal initiative to listen much more closely to the employees who were talking to customers every day.

An acceptance of failure as a necessary stepping-stone to success is an integral part of the culture of Silicon Valley. As a partner at Kleiner Perkins, one of the Valley's major VC firms, Kevin Compton met with industry leaders from other countries who were visiting the Valley in hopes of learning the secrets of its entrepreneurial magic. He would try to communicate the Valley gestalt with a story. "You're getting ready for your country's version of Thanksgiving dinner with the family. You're 32 years old, you have kids, and you're going to your in-laws' for dinner," says Compton. "After working at your version of IBM for ten years, everything was going great. But all of a sudden you left that job to go to a high-profile start-up that raised a whole bunch of money and completely flamed out 18 months later. I would ask these guys, 'Do you go to the family dinner?' They would usually say no. And I would tell them that in Silicon Valley, not only do you go to dinner, but your brother-in-law comes up and gives you a high five, saying, 'I wish I had the courage to do that.' As a risk taker, you got his attention. That's in our DNA."

This willingness to give it a shot and allow people a second, third, or fourth act in their careers has differentiated not only Silicon Valley's but also America's culture from that of other countries. Nokia researcher Henry Tirri says, "If I pose a question to a class of 100 students at a university in Finland, I'll get only one hand up, but I'll be totally convinced that the answer will be correct. If I do the same in the United States, I get 99 hands raised, out of which 90 are probably wrong. But they're willing to try."

Under the right leadership, even conservative government organizations like the Food and Drug Administration (FDA) can take informed risks and make a difference. When David Kessler became commissioner of the agency in 1990, processing of applications for new drug trials averaged 33 months—way too long a delay when lives are at stake. Kessler's response was to create a policy called Accelerated Approval. Then in 1996, when applications came in for protease inhibitors—a class of drugs that has radically boosted survival rates and improved the quality of life for those with HIV—they were approved within 47 days. "We set out a new policy, the industry cooperated, and it worked. We were transparent with the American people about the risks, and we ended up being right," he says. By the time Kessler left the FDA, 13 new antivirals had been approved that changed the course of a devastating disease.

Many gifted innovators are attracted to projects with a high probability of failure. "I *like* doing things that I am not sure will work out or not," says networking pioneer Paul Baran. "The element of risk adds excitement." Baran, who is still starting new companies at 80, is a stellar representative of America's scientific culture, with a willingness to venture where no man or woman has gone before.

The more successful you are, the more you have to lose, and the less likely you are to come up with disruptive innovation. But the failure *to* innovate often has a greater negative impact than the failure *of* innovation. The founders of Apple and FedEx, Steve Jobs and Fred Smith, have contrasting leadership styles and backgrounds, and are successful in completely different industries. But they share an eagerness to take bold yet calculated risks. Both survived very costly and public failures—Apple's Lisa computer; FedEx's ZapMail service—but that has not stopped them from pursuing grand new ideas with passion.

Openness

Innovation requires an open mind and an atmosphere that encourages people to imagine, think broadly, collaborate, capture serendipity, and have the freedom to create. Curiosity needs to be coupled with the ability to critically evaluate data, accept input, and be ready to adapt to change.

Lack of imagination kills many a project. At Zilog in the late 1970s, we developed a networked computer system that was years ahead of its time, nearly the equivalent of a PC running Microsoft Word. We demonstrated one of these machines to the management of Exxon, Zilog's main investor. Exxon, however, had also poured millions of dollars into typewriter companies that were developing dedicated word processors. Our group had a vision of the future, but Exxon's management couldn't imagine why anyone would want a general-purpose personal computer. As my former boss, Joe Kennedy, recalls, "They had already invested in these typewriters that they were calling word processors and said, 'Why do we need another one?' If Exxon had taken the time to understand what we had, Zilog could have beaten both Microsoft and Apple to market." Instead, Exxon passed, and many Zilog employees left to start their own companies. Silicon Valley is filled with successful new ventures launched by innovators who became entrepreneurs when their management would not consider new ideas.

Some of the most significant inventions in history—from penicillin, to Viagra, to Post-it Notes—were created because someone was open to looking beyond the original plan. Viagra was originally developed as a drug for hypertension. By paying attention to one of the compound's unanticipated side effects, Pfizer launched a new era of drugs that treat sexual dysfunction, and created one of its bestselling products. Capturing serendipity requires flexibility and being open to surprise. "The greatest innovations come from accepting that unknown chance in your life," says Yogen Dalal, managing director at Mayfield Fund. Without a culture of openness, deviations from plan are often covered up, instead of coming to light early so that the company can adapt.

Openly sharing information also creates pathways for valuable feedback. Some of the most costly failures in Silicon Valley were the result of projects that had been kept under wraps for too long. Roger McNamee, managing director of the private-equity firm Elevation Partners, points to the collapse of many early "pen computing" companies as the result of people "thinking they had something so incredible they couldn't show it to anybody. As a consequence, they never got feedback saying, 'Guys, this is stupid; you're making a brick with a pen that doesn't work.'"

There's a natural tension between openness and focus in all areas of innovation, especially in the development of products or programs. It's possible to be *too* open, always changing direction or specifications so that nothing gets done. But too much focus can overly constrain innovators. At the beginning of a project, when you are looking at needs, framing questions, and coming up with ideas, you want to encourage broad thinking and experimentation. Once a specific path has been agreed upon, it's time to execute and not constantly reformulate the solution or add "just one more" feature. But it's important to open your mind again when you are periodically assessing and making decisions as to how to proceed. Otherwise, you can end up with focused execution toward a goal that may no longer be the right one.

Microsoft, which began as a software tools company, ended up in the operating system business to meet the demands of a very large customer—IBM. "If Gates had sat down and said, 'No, I'm focused on tools,'" says entrepreneur Marc Andreessen, the coinventor of the Web browser, "someone else would have been Microsoft."

Patience

Patience is a mandatory condition if innovation is to thrive, and it doesn't have to be a passive process. Innovators need to be comfortable with abiding ambiguity for a time instead of jumping on the first idea or solution that comes along. They also require *active patience*: the tenacity to overcome technical obstacles and to champion their bold new ideas in the face of disbelief. Because of the persistence of Genentech's scientists, a drug called Avastin received FDA approval for treatment of colorectal cancer in 2004—15 years after the initial research began. You can have patience and still do business with a sense of urgency.

If a new technology requires a major change in infrastructure, the time and money that will be needed for it to become pervasive are substantially increased. "The automobile remains a plaything until you have a highway system. The telephone system didn't work unless we strung a million miles of wires," says former HP Labs director Joel Birnbaum. In such cases, it is particularly important to spend the time up front on research and experimentation so that the infrastructure is built around solutions that are right for the long term.

Leaders and financial backers need to have the patience to let ideas ripen. If they sense impatience, employees either will not take the time to try something new or will take the quickest path rather than the best. Projects and companies that might have produced great products and profits can be shut down as a result of lack of patient capital. In the late 1990s, 3Com was in a battle with Cisco for market share in the networking market. But the 3Com board demanded a faster path to profitability. "So we pulled out of the enterprise business," recalls 3Com's chairman, Eric Benhamou, "thus setting the company back five to ten years." The result was that few people today remember 3Com, while Cisco grew to dominate the networking market.

The time frames and measurement techniques that are appropriate for development efforts are not the same as those for research projects. "There are periods where you can't tell whether an individual thread is going to succeed," says David Clark, a senior research scientist at MIT who was instrumental in the development of the Internet. "You can't have some bean counter always looking over the wall with their clipboard saying, 'How are you doing?'"

Trust

As a company leader or financial backer, you must trust your people and the innovation process. Only with this foundation will employees and executives allow themselves to be vulnerable, take risks, and have the freedom to create. When trust erodes, horizons get pulled in as innovative potential is sacrificed to meet demonstrable milestones.

Innovators must trust themselves enough to push through obstacles and realize their vision of what could be, while still being open to new ideas and relentless self-assessment. Best Buy's Kal Patel calls this state of mind "living in the world of self-confidence *and* self-doubt." You have to both believe in your vision and be open to not believing at the same time, because trust without sufficient questioning can lead to disaster.

Each of the companies that I cofounded developed products that pushed the edge of technology and targeted markets that did not yet exist, as many start-ups do. Our early investors and employees had to trust in our vision. We, in turn, had to trust our small, select teams, giving them the freedom to execute the steps necessary for us to realize our dream. Entrepreneurship is all about trust.

Building partnerships around innovation requires extending trust beyond a single organization. Long-term partnerships, rather than project-by-project transactions, enable openness and sharing of information.

Genuine trust gives people the freedom to question. A start-up called Gavilan lost tens of millions of dollars of its investors' money in the 1980s by developing a portable computer boasting several technologies that were way ahead of their time, including a touch pad and an LCD display. Customers were lining up to buy this technical marvel; there was a $70 million backlog of orders. But the company tried to cram too many new technologies into the same machine and ended up with an unreliable product. "I was demoing the product to the secretary of the interior," recalls Wes Raffel, who was responsible for Gavilan's marketing and sales. "I had two machines with me, and both of them failed." No one was willing to stop and face the fact that the technology just wasn't ready for prime time. Eventually the company crashed, hitting the wall at 100 miles an hour, because it did not balance technical risk with honest self-assessment and accountability. But Raffel ended up learning a valuable lesson. "Gavilan's CEO had this magnetic personality and blind allegiance from his team," he says. "They all drank the Kool-Aid, and nobody was willing to say, 'Let's slow down.'"

AN INNOVATOR'S MIND IN ACTION: HAWKINS'S FOUR QUESTIONS

Jeff Hawkins is the brilliant scientist behind the Palm Pilot and the Handspring Treo. But his real passion is not for designing handheld devices. It's for understanding how we think. "When

I was a teenager, I made a list of the biggest questions I could muster," he recalls. "Why does the universe exist? Why are the laws of physics as they are? Why is there life, and where did it come from? And given life, what is intelligence? I stopped there, because it seemed to me that we might be able to solve my last question." If we understood how our own brains work, hoped Hawkins, we might be able to build tools that would help us answer the *first* three questions. At his father's suggestion, Hawkins studied electronics, and upon graduating from college, he took a job at Intel as an engineer. But he hadn't lost sight of his list of questions. He read an article in *Scientific American* written by biologist Francis Crick, the codiscoverer of DNA, which said that we were lacking a framework for understanding the brain. Hawkins decided to tackle the problem.

At Intel, he valiantly tried to convince his bosses and others in the tech industry that studying the brain could have enormous potential for advances in computing, but no one listened. Hawkins did not let this stop him. He quit his job and enrolled as a graduate student at UC Berkeley to study neuroscience, only to come up against more obstacles. "I wanted to study theories of the neocortex, but they said I couldn't do it as a graduate student," says Hawkins. "At that time there was nobody researching the area I was interested in, and they wouldn't let a graduate student pursue independent research. I had to work for somebody else on their project."

Eventually Hawkins decided that he would need to go back into business. "First of all, I had to put some bread on the table for my family. I wanted the financial resources to pursue my research," he says. He also realized that he needed to learn how to effect change at the institutional level, influencing decision makers to change their opinions. He wanted to make a name for himself so that he would have enough credibility to marshal the resources he needed to take on the big questions.

While working on the first tablet computer for a company called Grid, Hawkins got hooked on mobile computing and launched Palm in 1992. At first, the company almost didn't make it. A hardware partnership with Casio didn't work out, and the whole nascent mobile-computing industry seemed to be imploding. But one board member at Palm trusted Hawkins, and asked him if he knew what product people really wanted. Hawkins went home and designed the Palm Pilot that same night. The rest of the board thought he was crazy to want to build the whole product from scratch, including the operating system, the hardware, and the software. But this time he was able to convince others of the potential of his ideas. "We had $3 million, little support, and just 27 employees," he says. "We could have just died a slow death. But instead we said, 'Let's go for it.'"

With the spectacular success of the Palm Pilot, Hawkins finally gained the financial independence and credibility he needed to tackle his research. In 2002, he launched the Redwood Neuroscience Institute in Menlo Park, funding it himself and working with academic institutions like Stanford and Berkeley to realize his vision. In the next three years, over 120 scientists came to RNI, bringing their intelligence to bear on understanding the neocortex. "There was no other place like this, where you had unfettered energy focused on a particular scientific problem," says Hawkins.

Eventually Hawkins decided that if RNI could turn its theories into a workable technology, he could get more people involved in furthering his work. He cofounded a company called Numenta to build a tool set developed from the institute's new understandings of how the brain works. "Numenta may take four to five years to get to profitability," says Hawkins. "The keys to success will be going slowly, not getting ahead of ourselves, and not trying to be too big."

Hawkins embodies the core values of innovation. He has always been intensely curious, he is willing to take risks, he is open to change, and he is tenacious and patient, gaining the trust of others while never losing faith in his own vision.

THE PROCESS OF INNOVATION

There is no one predictable path to successful innovation. "Half of the great innovations in the world happened from great insights, the other half happened by accident, and none of them happened on a schedule," says long-time technology investor Roger McNamee. But behind the chaos there is a process: identifying a need and a set of questions to explore; trying and testing new ideas; and assessing whether to go forward or to return to generating more ideas, questions, or needs.

The innovation process is driven by the need to understand how something works or why it doesn't; to grow revenue, reduce costs, or increase productivity; to solve a customer's problem; or to keep people healthy and save lives. "If done well, this process of identifying and characterizing needs becomes the DNA of invention," says Paul Yock, a professor of bioengineering at Stanford. In business, the trick is to identify the needs of your potential customers before they do. "By the time your customers tell you they want something, it's too late," says Carol Bartz, executive chairman and former CEO of Autodesk.

By designing inexpensive and powerful software products like Quicken, QuickBooks, and TurboTax, Intuit has revolutionized the ways in which individuals and small businesses pay their bills and taxes, manage their accounting, and handle their payroll. At first, it seemed that the company could do no wrong. But when Intuit introduced eight new products that flopped between 1994 and 1999, founder Scott Cook was determined to find out why. Analyzing these failures, he was surprised to discover that the same employees, types of technology, brand names, distribution channels, and target customers were often involved in both the company's flops *and* its successes. The difference was that "the successful products addressed an important unsolved customer problem," he says. "Nobody had tried to solve the problem yet because they didn't see it. But suddenly we did. That required us to undergo a mindset change, so that we could see a different paradigm from what we and others had believed."

Even noncommercial organizations can think in terms of their "customers" whose needs must be met. For an academic institution, the customer is society at large—the people and organizations that leverage the institution's research and hire its students. Government organizations must be clear about the evolving needs of the country's citizens as changes in demographics, economics, or foreign affairs affect defense, education, health care, and business policies. Funding agencies can learn to allocate their funds more effectively by viewing the recipients of their grants as their customers, understanding how best to enable the grantees to do their research, enhance their education, launch businesses, or lead productive, independent lives.

Behind each need is a set of questions to explore. *Is there a better way of doing this? What if we . . . ? How does this work? Why doesn't this work? What does the customer really need? What will the problem look like 10 years from now?* Learning how to frame the right questions is not easy. Asking a customer, "What features do you want in this product?" is certain to evoke a much more limited set of answers than, "What problems are you trying to solve?" Going a step further to understand the specific requirements and constraints of an application enables innovators to anticipate the customer's unarticulated needs as well, which can lead to even more significant innovation. Questions can also be employed to add useful constraints to a project. There are times when it is important to focus on a specific problem and times when you want to encourage broad exploration.

Our ongoing struggle in Iraq is a disastrous example of the importance of framing questions correctly. We went to war with the technology to support a precision military campaign with minimal casualties. But we had the answers to the wrong problem. The military was prepared for a soldierless attack, but occupying a country requires boots on the ground. We were not prepared technologically, financially, or emotionally for the actual problem we're faced with now.

Brainstorming for *ideas*—new ways to address perceived needs—is often thought of as the "magic" part of innovation. It takes the right combination of research, creativity, and enough time to think. Once a promising set of ideas has been identified, it's time to *try and test* them through market research, scientific experimentation, or prototyping, at which point methodology and discipline become crucial.

Think back to your high school science classes when you learned how to design experiments. My son and I spent an afternoon firing a Nerf bow and arrow down the hallway for a high school physics assignment. After several hours of shooting arrows and calculating the propulsive force of the string, our results were inconclusive. Though we had fun, the longest section of David's lab report dealt with margins of error, because we didn't have the tools to accurately measure the arrows' trajectory or the force of the string. Lesson learned: experimental design is critical. Deciding how to test, where to get feedback, and critical analysis of data are all key to successful experimentation.

The Internet has transformed the relationship between companies and their customers, opening up direct and unfiltered channels of communication that were unimaginable in previous eras, and providing companies with instant access to feedback and ideas from their customer base. With this free flow of information also comes the burden of filtering out the relevant information from the noise. Focus groups are useful only if you're asking the right questions of the right people; as Henry Ford put it, if he had asked his customers what they wanted, they would have said a faster horse. If an idea is significantly ahead of its time, early market feedback can be misleading. You have to decide whether you believe strongly enough in the concept to risk taking the next step *in spite of* not getting positive feedback.

Once the testing is done and the data have been analyzed, *honest self-assessment* is required. Does the proposed solution really answer the question at hand? Is the anticipated need significant enough to justify moving forward? Is it necessary to go back and test more, try another idea, or reframe the questions? The journey from the initial idea to success may take only weeks or months for a new product feature. But the development and testing of a new drug or a paradigm-shifting product can go on for years or decades.

Reed Hastings launched Netflix in 1998 as a frustrated video renter who was tired of paying late fees. The company started with a single-rental model: users paid $4 to rent a single DVD for a week, plus a $2 shipping and handling charge. "It was just not a *wow*," admits Hastings in retrospect. "It was OK, but we needed a wow to break through." Looking harder at the business, he concluded that a monthly subscription model—with the addition of a "dynamic queue" so that customers could always have a DVD to watch and more to look forward to— might just work. Netflix relaunched in September 1999, and this time it was a *wow*.

It can take multiple cycles of brainstorming, testing, analyzing, and adapting to get a project right—or to sensibly call it quits. The process involved in innovation is often like riding a unicycle. To balance and keep moving ahead, you have to pedal both backward and forward.

ORTHOGONAL INNOVATION

The innovation process can result in life-changing break-throughs or incremental improvements to existing ideas or products. There is a third type of significant innovation that comes from applying existing technologies in new ways. I call this *orthogonal* innovation.

The iPod is a great example. Apple was not the first company to offer a portable MP3 player, downloadable music, or software that allows users to "rip" and "burn" CDs. But the iPod packaged existing technological elements in an easy-to-use fashion. The integration of the elegantly designed physical device with the iTunes software is what shook the foundations of the music industry, opened up new markets for Apple, and enhanced all of our lives. "It was not just engineering, or downloading music, or third-party peripherals, or even the marketing," says Jon Rubinstein, the former engineering vice president at Apple who oversaw the development of the device. "It was all of them combined, plus the retail stores where people got to actually handle an iPod for themselves. It all played really well together. The iPod was a product we all wanted. It was something we were all passionate about. But when we started, I never envisioned that it would sell 100 million."

In fact, the vertical integration that many analysts saw as Apple's core weakness turned out to be the factor that enabled the company to turn the iPod into a company-defining mile-stone success. Apple took the unique approach of looking at downloadable music as an entire system—complete with copy protection to appease the recording industry's concerns—rather than just another new gadget or Web site. Apple leveraged the Internet to provide users with a great music *experience*, rather than just the ability to play MP3 files.

The credit card was introduced in the 1920s as a quicker and easier way for the growing number of automobile owners to buy gas. As companies like Diners Club and American Express made it possible to purchase meals, lodging, and merchandise with a swipe of the plastic, the concept of the credit card became a hugely disruptive innovation. The *debit* card, on the other hand, was an orthogonal innovation. It used the same basic technology as the credit card, with a different business model, to provide services that we now take for granted, but that we would not have thought to ask for before they became available.

Breakthroughs take time to be widely adopted. Incremental and orthogonal innovations typically have a more immediate impact. It is important to have the right balance of all three types of innovation. Breakthrough and orthogonal ideas and products can initiate new market cycles, driving opportunities for significant growth, whereas incremental innovations keep each cycle going.

NO BIGGER THAN A JAZZ BAND

If you talk to anyone who is in a leadership position, that person will tell you that attracting and retaining the best talent are top priority. What does this mean in the context of innovation?

The best talent embodies the five core values and has the right combination of aptitude, skill, judgment, passion, and drive. Such people's curiosity and openness to new experience are as important as their pedigree. They require deep understanding to garner respect, a sense of infectious excitement to rally the organization around them, and an almost compulsive drive to tinker. "What we always looked for were people who were born with soldering irons in their hands," says Jon Rubinstein. "People with a passion for products, for the creation process, and for technology itself."

Many innovators do not have a firm idea of what obstacles they will face when they launch something new. They have a certain dose of naïveté that prevents them from being daunted by the problems that inevitably lie ahead. Reid Hoffman, founder of the LinkedIn social network, has personally mentored many of the founders of start-ups like Facebook, Flickr, and Digg. In the late 1990s, he joined PayPal and ended up being responsible for all of PayPal's external relationships, including coping with banking regulations. "By not knowing about government regulations, banking, fraud, financial structure, and a whole bunch of other things," says Hoffman, "we basically ran out into the middle of a minefield, not even knowing that there *were* minefields. But once we were there, the only thing we could do was to go forward—and we pulled it off, while most of the people in the banking industry were sitting on the sidelines." Akin to this naïveté is a sense of play, even in the midst of very demanding work. "I have a category of people in my network who really enjoy playing with technology," says Hoffman. "They start with an artifact and say, 'What can I make out of this?' This is different from goal-driven behavior."

Magic happens when small groups of the most talented people have a sense of purpose and shared values, are provided with sufficient resources, and are empowered to come up with something great. Even for complex projects that ultimately may require significant resources to implement, the initial teams should be kept small, cutting down on communication overhead and ensuring that the group can change direction quickly if necessary.

In Silicon Valley, the optimal size of these groups is often described by the "two-pizza" rule, which says that nothing amazing ever happens in a group that can't be fed by two pizzas. Nokia researcher Henry Tirri refers to the right size of these groups as "no larger than a jazz band," so that individuals can improvise and play off of one another without requiring a conductor to stand before them, orchestrating every move.

Every jazz aficionado knows that the best bands are made up not just of musicians who can play killer solos, but of those who know how to listen to one another and serve the collective vision of the music. Particularly now, when products and projects often call upon a broad range of expertise, finding team members who know how to collaborate with one another—and with the world at large—is crucial. Increasingly, leaders are recognizing the value of what IDEO, a leading product design company, calls *T-shaped people*—those who have a depth of knowledge in a particular area, but also the breadth to communicate well with people in other disciplines.

It wasn't just the technology of Apple's iPhone that made it a landmark product that grew the market for smart phones generally. It was also the elegant and imaginative product design, and a marketing team that knew how to build public expectation into a frenzy. Innovation grows out of the combination of diverse sets of expertise. Facilitating communication between the various groups, and creating the right balance of rewards for all, requires leadership that understands and appreciates the importance of the entire cast of characters.

"There are half a dozen words in the English language that are substitutes for *substance*. Three of them are *innovation, accountability,* and *leadership*," says retired Intel CEO Andy Grove. "Companies that let people get away with murder talk too much about accountability. Those that don't have the courage to leave the handrail talk incessantly about leadership.

And people who are incapable of changing what they are doing, or even analyzing what's wrong, go on and on about innovation." Innovation is not just another pat phrase with little meaning beyond the latest hot start-up. We need real, sustainable innovation, which can come only with courage on the part of leadership and an Ecosystem that is in balance.

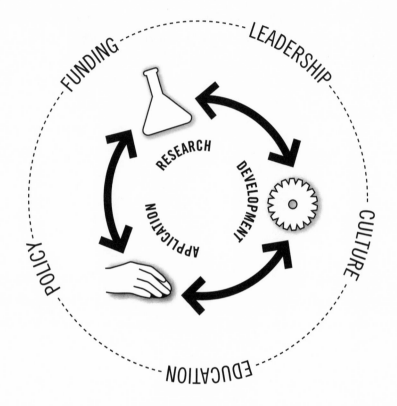

CHAPTER 2

THE INNOVATION
ECOSYSTEM

I couldn't possibly keep track of my life without my "sticky notes." The story of how Post-its came to be is a classic tale of the communities of the Innovation Ecosystem collaborating to develop a world-changing product from a serendipitous discovery.

In 1968, a scientist named Spence Silver at 3M's lab in Minneapolis was researching ways to make the company's tape-based adhesives stronger. He failed to find what he was looking for, but instead he stumbled on something new: an adhesive that was strong enough to stick to many surfaces but could be easily removed and reused. Silver could have just moved on to try other ways of developing a stronger adhesive. But as a researcher in a lab that permitted a certain amount of open-ended exploration, he was not constrained by a predetermined outcome, and he was intrigued by the potential of his accidental invention.

Silver spent the next five years prototyping different forms of glue and working with others in the company to figure out how his discovery could be turned into successful products. Then one day, a scientist in 3M's product development department named Art Fry felt frustrated because the bookmarks kept falling out of his hymnal in church, and remembered hearing something about Silver's temporary adhesive. He wondered if it could be used to create bookmarks that would stay put until you no longer needed them.

Transforming Silver's discovery and Fry's notion into the Post-it Notes we use today was not a painless process. Many naysayers in the company said things along the way like, "Who would pay for a little scrap of paper?" But Fry was tenacious in his pursuit, and 3M's leadership was supportive.

When Post-its finally hit the market in 1977, they didn't catch on immediately. Consumers couldn't imagine why they would need the product until 3M decided to widely distribute free samples. Once people saw how these versatile little sticky notes could be used, their imaginations ran wild. The Post-it brand is now a family of products for people of all ages to use at work, at home, and at school—including digital Post-it software for personal computers that uses no adhesive at all.

These all-important multicolored pieces of paper are a result of a thriving Innovation Ecosystem: Silver's research, which led to the discovery of a new form of glue; Fry's brainstorm to develop a line of Post-it products; and consumers who are continually finding new uses for them to this day. 3M's leadership understood the fundamentals of innovation and provided the right environment for talented, persistent employees to work together.

NATURAL INNOVATION

In the foothills west of Stanford University, there are 1,500 acres of land used for research in environmental restoration and habitat conservation. The locals have nicknamed this beautiful area "the Dish" after the radio telescope that sits at the top of the hill. For us, it is a prime recreation site for hiking and jogging. Each day, as I walk my familiar trail around the Dish, I am surrounded by nature's own restless creativity.

Trees, grasses, and wild mustard blanket the hills—golden brown in the heat of the summer, turning to a beautiful green and yellow after the rains come in the fall and new growth starts to appear in the spring. Hawks circle overhead, looking for food. Squirrels are everywhere, having grown comfortable with people in their midst. Snakes, lizards, gophers, jackrabbits, deer, bobcats, and the occasional mountain lion also consider the reserve their home. And among all of the wildlife are other people like me, walking and talking about personal, professional, or global problems, rain or shine, inspired by gorgeous views of the Stanford campus and Silicon Valley. Last summer, a fire burned 128 acres of the area, destroying plants and chasing away the inhabitants. But within weeks, with special care and nurturing by conservation biologists from the university, life on the Dish began to revive.

The Dish is an ecosystem: a dynamic interaction of living communities and their environment, working together to transfer the energy and nutrients necessary for survival. Every single tree that I pass is a living network unto itself, and the 1,500-acre reserve is only a small part of the larger ecosystem of the Bay Area. An ecosystem can be as narrow as a single stream or as wide as an ocean, but in all cases, ecosystems fail if they are not in balance, with the right environmental factors to support the species living within them.

The Innovation Ecosystem is made up of communities of people with different types of expertise and skill sets. Scientists, administrators, business leaders, engineers, writers, educators, health-care professionals, and other individuals all play a role. Each community must receive the nutrients it deserves through leadership, funding, and public attention.

Just as the health of a single tree in the Dish is dependent upon on the health of the ecosystem of the whole Bay Area, so the Innovation Ecosystem of any particular business or group relies on the broader environment for innovation in the country and in the world. The various inhabitants of an Innovation Ecosystem can be classified into three communities: *research, development,* and *application.*

Activity in the research community benefits the entire Ecosystem in its quest for new knowledge; it is typically classified on a spectrum that runs from "basic" to "applied." Basic research thrives when the fewest external constraints are placed upon it. The search to understand the relationship between electricity and magnetism and the study of genetics and heredity are two examples of basic research that became critical building blocks for future innovations. Louis Pasteur, who developed the germ theory of disease, once remarked that "in the field of observation, chance favors only the prepared mind." Basic research prepares the mind of the scientific community as a whole and creates an environment for discovery.

Applied research, on the other hand, is framed by defining a particular problem to be solved. The invention of the transistor to replace expensive vacuum tubes was a triumph of applied research. The ongoing hunt for a specific set of genes that increases a child's chances of being born with autism is another example of applied research that is building on the discoveries of basic science. Although consideration of a potential market may play a role in applied research, addressing a specific business need is usually the role of the development community.

Researchers typically enjoy exploring the ambiguity of broad unanswered questions. They get positive feedback from the challenges of the process itself, sharing ideas and peer recognition. In view of its crucial role in the Ecosystem, research should be judged not by the number of patents obtained, but by the amount of new knowledge brought into the world by scientists, and by former students providing the foundation for innovation in other communities.

In a world that increasingly values commercial endeavors more highly than the quest for scientific knowledge, the importance of basic research is often taken for granted or forgotten entirely. What is often called corporate research is usually just advanced technological development, constrained by the needs of a specific business rather than being motivated by a desire to further general understanding. It does not benefit the rest of the Ecosystem in the same ways that the research community does, and it should not be seen as a substitute.

In the natural ecosystem of a tree, the branches and leaves won't get any water without a well-developed root system. In the Innovation Ecosystem, without a thriving research community at the roots, long-term, sustainable advancement is not possible.

The development community brings ideas to market; it includes the engineers, designers, marketers, and salespeople who turn new discoveries into usable (and hopefully user-friendly) products and services. A Pfizer scientist could leverage the discovery of a hormone that modulates insulin into a revolutionary drug for treating diabetes. Product developers may fashion new concepts from already-existing technologies, such as packaging a pregnancy test so that it's convenient for home use or creating a software application for organizing digital photos. Engineers may refine production methods toward a goal of greater efficiency, as those at Intel have been doing for decades at chip fabrication plants.

Those in the development community want to build something great and tend to favor breadth over depth. Rather than working on the same problem set for a decade, they are often anxious to move on and tackle the next challenge. Their rewards come from translating ideas into products, recognition of their contributions, and the positive feedback gained from seeing these products in use.

After one particularly frustrating meeting at Packet Design, chief scientist Van Jacobson observed that it was as if the researchers and developers were speaking different languages. The developers were like rock climbers—they wanted to find the tallest mountain and were excited about climbing to the top as quickly as possible. The researchers were like cartographers—their goal in climbing a mountain was to gain a better perspective of what interesting terrain lay ahead. This was an essential insight for us as a company. In understanding the perspectives of the different scientists and engineers, we could play to each person's strength and enable him or her to work better as a member of the team.

The application community drives activity throughout the Ecosystem by bringing science or technology to bear on the needs of individuals and organizations. In touch with the day-to-day needs of the world at large, the members of this community provide crucial information for researchers looking for problems to solve and developers navigating a swiftly changing technological landscape.

These are the scientists who choose to be internists, surgeons, or psychiatrists, doing clinical work as opposed to research in a lab. They're the engineers or developers who enable users to take advantage of what technology has to offer or the individuals who use the latest technological gadget to organize their lives. The application community is on the front lines of innovation, because it's not the mere existence of a technology, but rather the adoption of it, that creates change.

For Google to become the tech powerhouse that it is today required more than turning academic research on new algorithms into a nifty new search engine for the Web. The company also had to develop a business model that would provide it with a steady source of income for the long term. Google's

AdWords program—which displays unobtrusive paid advertisements alongside the algorithm's trustworthy search results—has proved to be as innovative and effective as the search engine itself. Furthermore, Google's application of state-of-the-art IT strategies to implement its widely distributed "cloud" of data centers has provided the necessary technical foundation for the ever-increasing scale of its business. Smart research, development, and application have all played indispensable roles in Google's success.

The sustainability of our national Innovation Ecosystem will depend upon maintaining a healthy balance between all three communities. We need a bold and well-funded research community to discover new knowledge and ideas looking far into the future. We need a prolific development community to make advances in the production and delivery of products and services. And we need a thriving application community to bring these advances to people throughout the world.

A well-balanced Ecosystem will be required to address the most serious challenges that we now face as a society. Reducing our dependence on oil and reversing the trends in climate change will require companies and individuals to find ways to conserve energy and use less petroleum-based fuel. We will need new kinds of hybrid cars, more efficient appliances, and groundbreaking ways of moderating energy demand. At the same time, we need to invest in basic and applied research to discover new sustainable energy sources and lessen our impact on the environment.

As in a natural ecosystem like the Dish, boosting the health of any part of the Innovation Ecosystem increases the vigor and adaptability of the whole. Organizations that reach outside of their primary community to tap the intelligence and resources of all three are leading the way to sustainable innovation.

AN INTERESTING EXPERIMENT

The Genomics Institute of the Novartis Research Foundation (GNF) is a new model for interdisciplinary research. Founded in 1999 with funding from the Swiss pharmaceutical giant, GNF focuses on solving complex medical problems by integrating advances in chemistry, biology, automation, and IT. Its passionate leader, Peter Schultz, is a unique combination of academic researcher and entrepreneur. He has cofounded seven start-ups, and is also a chemistry professor at the Scripps Research Institute in La Jolla, California.

The catalyst for the creation of GNF was the hope that the time required for drug discovery could be dramatically accelerated through the use of new techniques that enable genomics labs to conduct thousands of experiments in parallel, instead of analyzing one gene or molecule at a time. The typical investors in a biotech start-up would not have had the patience to fund the group as it explored various ways of accomplishing this. But Novartis took a longer view and funded GNF as a separate entity, enabling Schultz to attract scientists who have the skills to both build new technology platforms and apply them to the development of new products.

Schultz modestly describes GNF as "an interesting experiment" in building bridges between academia, the private sector, and basic and applied research. Some of the institute's programs are purely exploratory, but it also has the resources and expertise to develop practical health-care applications. "We have attracted people who are not afraid to go into new areas or assimilate ideas and data from a lot of different fields," says Schultz.

GNF is a provocative hybrid model for research: an independent lab that has the freedom to pursue basic science, while also having the wherewithal to translate its discoveries into products. It is an experiment that is working because of a synergistic combination of visionary leadership, world-class talent, and patient financial backing.

INTUITIVE DEVELOPMENT

Determining the right trade-offs among technology, cost, and customer requirements is a key challenge for the development community. Companies that strike the right balance, like Intuitive Surgical, can really make a difference.

Most surgical operations today are performed with instruments that require an incision large enough to wedge a surgeon's hands into the body. *Laparoscopic,* or minimally invasive surgery—a huge medical advance of the 1980s—reduced the size of the incision, but the instruments were hard to use and did not have the range of motion of a surgeon's hand. Thus, while medical advances for procedures that involve the removal of an entire organ were made quickly, the state of the art for operations that require more delicate work stayed stagnant for a long time. Improving the clinical outcomes of these more complex operations was the development target of a start-up called Intuitive Surgical, based in Silicon Valley. The company has revolutionized medicine with a robotic system for assisting surgery called the da Vinci.

The da Vinci system is designed for maximum flexibility, with a wristlike mechanism that allows it to function like a human hand. The surgeon sits at a large console, viewing the patient through a 3D display, while maneuvering the instruments with precision hand controls. Computers embedded in the device make these movements feel completely natural to the surgeon, dramatically reducing training time. "It's like doing a normal operation," says company president Gary Guthart. "You see what you want, and you move to go get it—but it has the benefits of minimally invasive surgery to the patient." When I visited the company's headquarters, Guthart took me into the demo room to show me just how intuitive the process really is. To my surprise, I was able to manipulate the instruments within minutes.

In the mid-1980s, a physician and entrepreneur named Fred Moll visited the Stanford Research Institute for a demo of computer-aided surgery, which was part of a research program funded by DARPA and the National Institutes of Health (NIH). Able to foresee the potential impact of the technology, Moll licensed it in 1995 and launched Intuitive Surgical, hiring some of the original SRI researchers, including Gary Guthart.

Developing the da Vinci required the evolution of several different technologies in parallel. The robotics component is based on tools developed in the 1950s and 1960s for handling hazardous materials. The video component and the use of insufflation—the technique of injecting gas to expand the body cavity—came from refinements made in laparoscopic surgery. Research into virtual-reality displays and navigating immersive environments also played a role. Advancements in high-resolution imagery and optics were critical to ensuring that the surgeon experiences the operation just as if he or she were standing over the patient.

The company stumbled several times on its road to success. Getting the da Vinci ready required integrating more than 3,000 microcomponents and having them function seamlessly together. Commercially available endoscopy turned out to be inadequate for the company's imaging needs, so it had to develop its own video technology. Early ideas about how da Vinci could be incorporated into the routines of an operating room had to be scrapped.

But once the system became available, surgeons not only embraced it but found new ways to use it. A doctor in Germany suggested that da Vinci might be ideal for performing prostate operations. Soon he was training other surgeons in the procedure, and now 70 percent of all prostate operations are performed using the system. Patients needing gastric bypasses, hysterectomies, and mitral-valve repair have also benefited from less invasive operations and shorter recovery times.

After becoming the first robotic system for laparoscopic surgery approved by the FDA, da Vinci is now employed in more than 600 operating rooms, and the company has a $5 billion market cap. Yogen Dalal, an early investor in the company, says, "If you look at their system, it wasn't incremental in any way. It was completely and totally disruptive."

Intuitive Surgical is an excellent example of cross-pollination between the research, development, and application communities. DARPA-funded research inspired the launch of a product start-up that collaborated with its customers to apply radical new technology to save lives.

ABSOLUTELY, POSITIVELY INNOVATIVE

At midnight the planes begin arriving from all over the world, and by 2 a.m. the last one has departed. For two hours, the main FedEx hub in Memphis is filled with activity—unloading, sorting, and then reloading the planes. Achieving almost perfect service levels as FedEx transports millions of packages a day throughout the world by air and ground requires an enormous amount of discipline and attention to process. But from the day the company was founded by Fred Smith, FedEx has not wavered from its commitment to applying technology to best serve its customers.

It has developed new noise-suppression technology for aircraft, and partnered with the University of Maryland to produce heads-up displays that improve safety and enable pilots to land in limited-visibility conditions. The company designs new ways of making its transport vehicles more fuel-efficient and safe, with onboard cameras and sensors. Advanced operations research allows FedEx to optimally schedule flight times, truck routes, and deliveries; and new sorting technologies automate the flow of packages efficiently. The company's commitment to leading in IT has grown out of Smith's realization that, as he puts it, "Information about a package is as important as delivery of the package itself."

One of the company's most visible innovations is its Web site, fedex.com, which today is used to ship more than 1 million packages daily and track more than 5 million more. It saves FedEx millions of dollars, and customers avoid the time and frustration of waiting on hold to talk to a customer service representative.

An interactive Web site that brings a business closer to its customers seems commonplace today. But in 1994, when the company registered the fedex.com domain name, it was not. FedEx was one of the first commercial companies to use the Web for something other than repurposing marketing brochures. We are now accustomed to companies such as Amazon, Yahoo, eBay, Google, Facebook, and LinkedIn that have leveraged the Internet to enable new business and consumer applications. Few remember that the first wave of Internet early adopters was primarily academic researchers looking for a way to share information faster and more widely.

At a 1994 briefing on future technologies, Bill Joy, Sun Microsystems' cofounder and a technical visionary, spent most of the day talking about the ramifications of the Internet and a new technology called the World Wide Web that had been developed at CERN in Switzerland. Rob Carter, FedEx's CIO, left the meeting knowing that the company had to have a presence on the Internet, but he wasn't quite sure in what way, so he asked IT director Miley Ainsworth to learn more.

Always keen to play with the latest technology, Ainsworth flew to Silicon Valley for a class at Stanford on HTML, the coding language of the Web. He came back with a copy of Mosaic, the first easy-to-use Web browser, developed by Marc Andreessen, then a student at the University of Illinois. Ainsworth figured that customers visiting FedEx's Web site would want to do more than just read an advertisement for the company's services, so he furnished the site with a simple form that said, "Enter your tracking number here to track a package." Once the company connected its Web software to its back-end databases, anyone with a browser was able to see if a package had been delivered without picking up the phone.

Enthusiasm for this new way of doing business spread rapidly throughout the company by word of mouth. The news that packages could be tracked at fedex.com spread virally through the emerging Internet. "It was an overnight sensation that quickly got a good reputation," Carter said. "It saved money. It was flexible. Its benefits were clear to us and were quickly recognized by our customers as well."

The site has grown far beyond even Ainsworth's hopes for it. Today more customers rely on fedex.com than use the company's 800 number. It has become a comprehensive interface to doing business with the company. FedEx's early embrace of the Web would not have been possible without the core values of innovation thriving at the company, and without close interaction between all of the communities of the Ecosystem.

CROSS-POLLINATING THE FUTURE

Each of these organizations demonstrates the importance of the individual communities of the Ecosystem, as well as the power resulting from the right flow of questions, knowledge, and technology between them. Researchers and developers benefit from having access to real-world data, and private industry is kept vital by having a steady stream of ideas and talent from labs.

Usually research inspires the development of products that are used in innovative applications. But end users often discover applications that developers never dream of, and research can result from a desire to understand more about how current products work. "Most of the original engines were developed by people without a knowledge of the relationship between heat and mechanical energy," says Joel Birnbaum, retired senior vice president at Hewlett-Packard, "but once the science of thermodynamics evolved to explain why engines had different efficiencies, it became possible to make great advances in engine design."

Organizations need people who are capable of translating among the three branches of the Ecosystem. Engineers and scientists working on advanced technology provide a critical bridge between the research and development communities. Those working in development may not have the time, the type of education, or the training to cull the information they require from advanced research. Resources are also needed to provide a bridge from the application community to development—people who probe the capabilities of new technologies and products, studying their potential impact on the organization.

As we look to address growing concerns over potential conflicts of interest arising between pharmaceutical companies and doctors or energy companies funding academic research, we must make sure that we do not stop the free flow of information between the communities of the Ecosystem that exerts a synergistic effect on innovation.

NURTURING THE INNOVATIVE ENVIRONMENT

Just as plants require water and sunlight if they are to grow, sustaining innovation requires the right *leadership, funding, policy, education,* and *culture.*

Business, political, and individual leadership all have an impact on the Ecosystem. Nurturing innovation in any organization is ultimately the responsibility of those at the top. "I have to ensure that we are a company that allows room for innovation and rewards it," says Disney CEO Bob Iger. "A big established company can still innovate. It is incumbent on the leadership not only to figure out how that can happen, but to make sure that it does happen." Company leaders and board members need to instill the capacity for change in their organizations and communicate a sense of shared mission to all employees.

Our nation's leaders decisively influence the health of the country's Innovation Ecosystem. Politicians influence day-to-day business processes through laws and regulations. They control funding and policy that directly affect our educational system and the research community. "How much a country invests in research will determine its business cycles two or three decades out," says Cisco CEO John Chambers.

Parents, educators, and the media are responsible for developing and inspiring the next generation of American innovators. Each of us, as an employee or a member of society, has the responsibility to lead within our own sphere of influence.

Competition for funding can bring out the best in innovators, but it can have the opposite impact if the resources are *too* scarce. It is not just the magnitude of funds that is important, but also how they are allocated. Stability and consistency of resources are critical for projects that span long periods of time.

"The government funded the development of the Internet for roughly 24 years, which is stunningly remarkable for any program like that," says Vint Cerf, now Google's chief Internet evangelist. "That sustained funding made a huge difference." If funding cannot be relied upon, innovators and leaders end up spending more time fund-raising than they spend working. This holds true for research grants, venture capital for entrepreneurs, or internal funding in larger organizations. Requirements to demonstrate progress too frequently can lead to short-term trade-offs.

Federal and state policies have a significant impact on the Ecosystem. Legislation, SEC regulations, litigation rules, healthcare requirements, and tax incentives all affect the ability of businesses to innovate effectively.

Education is equally important. We are all born with the potential to innovate. Kids are naturally curious, open-minded, trusting, and persistent. K-12 and higher education can develop this naturally innovative spirit or stifle it. The quality and accessibility of higher education influence the talent pool available to drive innovation throughout the Ecosystem.

The larger cultural context also makes a significant impact on our capacity for change. The promise of achieving the American Dream set the tone for entrepreneurialism and innovation in this country. The implicit values of our organizations and our nation can either reinforce or dilute the core values of innovation.

A complex shift in these environmental factors has thrown America's Innovation Ecosystem off balance, threatening the way of life that we now take for granted. Should we accept the idea that the United States is in decline as an economic power and that there's nothing we can do about it? Can we leave it up to capitalism, assuming that this shift is just a cycle that will be taken care of by the markets? No. To regain our balance will require everyone's focus. People and organizations must work on the problem from the bottom up, while demanding that our legislators take the lead on issues that require their involvement.

We must all think about the consequences for innovation of our business and policy decisions. If we don't, America is in danger of losing its Innovation Ecosystem completely—and thus, its leadership role in the emerging global economy.

First, we have to understand how we got to this point. For decades, our industries, government agencies, and universities produced a wealth of life-changing products and services, as well as a steady stream of people who were well prepared and eager to innovate in a wide range of fields. What happened to the brave nation that dared to put a man on the moon, launch a worldwide communications network, and crack the genetic code?

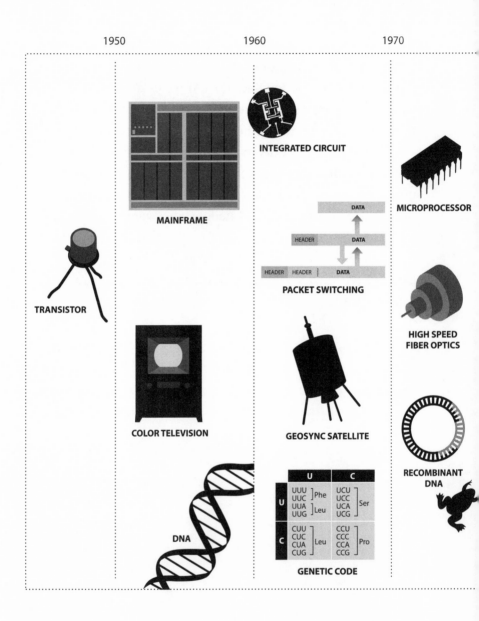

1950   1960   1970

INTEGRATED CIRCUIT

MAINFRAME

MICROPROCESSOR

DATA

HEADER   DATA

HEADER   HEADER   DATA

PACKET SWITCHING

TRANSISTOR

HIGH SPEED
FIBER OPTICS

COLOR TELEVISION

GEOSYNC SATELLITE

RECOMBINANT
DNA

	U	C
U	UUU UUC]Phe UUA UUG]Leu	UCU UCC UCA UCG]Ser
C	CUU CUC CUA CUG]Leu	CCU CCC CCA CCG]Pro

DNA

GENETIC CODE

CHAPTER 3

INSPIRATIONAL INNOVATION

I took a tour of Silicon Valley's Computer History Museum with my parents and my son a few years ago. The first areas of the exhibit represented the earliest days of computing, when my mother's and father's careers began. I grew up hearing stories about the Institute for Advanced Studies in Princeton, where my father worked with mathematician John von Neumann in the early 1950s as part of the team that built the first stored-program computer.

There in front of me at the museum was von Neumann's original system, built from vacuum tubes, along with the other early machines inspired by his architecture, which still influences the way computers are designed today. The first mainframes—which my parents helped design—were just glorified calculators by today's standards, but each one took up 1,000 square feet of space, or half a tennis court.

Midway through the exhibit, we reached the 1970s—the age of minicomputers, when I embarked on my own networking career. The transistor, first built in 1948, replaced large, power-hungry tubes. Then in 1958 came the integrated circuit, which put multiple transistors on a single silicon chip. These inventions allowed computers to shrink to the size of refrigerators. From integrated circuits were born the microprocessors that powered the very first truly personal computers, like the Apple IIs and Tandy TRS80s that we used to write the business plan for our first company, Bridge Communications.

We then strolled past the highly sophisticated PCs and workstations that launched the home computing revolution and created the online world. Finally, we reached an exhibit that David recognized—the portable desktops and laptops that he and his friends view as an integral part of their lives. These sleek, lightweight machines are orders of magnitude more powerful than my father and his contemporaries could have imagined in 1950.

Walking through the museum, I couldn't help but be struck by the incredible level of innovation in the second half of the twentieth century. The communications field was energized by the power of connecting individual computers together into networks located in a single office or on different sides of the planet. The development of cost-effective fiber optics and the Web brought these advances to consumers worldwide as the lines between computing, communications, and consumer electronics blurred.

This golden era of innovation went far beyond computing and communications. The medical world was transformed by the widespread use of antibiotics and vaccinations. The discovery of DNA and gene splicing gave birth to a whole new industry—biotechnology—that created much more effective ways of developing and testing new drugs. New food additives boosted production capacity and prolonged shelf life, while creating research opportunities for scientists as they studied the long-term impacts of these additives on health and the environment.

Burgeoning advances in the field of astronomy brought us a deeper understanding of the mechanics of the solar system, pulsars, and black holes. As petroleum became a critical resource for energy, it also provided the basis for a generation of synthetic materials, including plastics, solvents, and detergents. Meanwhile, the earth sciences saw advances in our understanding of earthquakes, weather, and the impact of technology and human behavior on global climate change.

THE ENDLESS FRONTIER

What was going on in America in the mid-twentieth century that brought about this wealth of new ideas and new technologies? Was there something in the water? Metaphorically speaking, there was. The core values of questioning, risk taking, openness, patience, and trust were nurtured by our nation's leadership, and they transformed our culture.

From radar to mass-produced penicillin and the atomic bomb, science played a significant role in the outcome of World War II. Scientists and engineers commanded the respect of the country's leaders and citizens. The abundance of new inventions resulting from government funding, such as the Internet, did not just benefit the military. These inventions also drove economic growth. The emergence of venture capital financing and entrepreneurial communities in places like Silicon Valley turned ideas into world-changing products.

World War II and the threats of the ensuing Cold War ensured that science was a national priority and provided the motivation to enlist the country's scientific community in the collective effort. But motivation alone was not enough. It also took vision and persistence, personified by Dr. Vannevar Bush. As a young professor at Tufts University in the early 1900s, Bush cofounded a radio tube company and later designed the mechanical calculators that were the precursors to digital computers.

The U.S. government had not been particularly focused on encouraging science and technology in the prewar era, but faced with the challenges of fighting the Nazis, President Roosevelt turned to experts for help. He put Dr. Bush in charge of the new Office of Scientific Research and Development, which coordinated the efforts of civilian scientists and the military during the war. Prompted by the terrifying possibility that the German army would develop the atomic bomb before the Allies did, Dr. Bush launched the Manhattan Project.

Dr. Bush's contributions to innovation had a lasting influence on policy. His office operated in new ways, forging relationships with scientists and engineers in industry and research labs throughout the country. This created job opportunities that encouraged a generation of scientists and engineers. My father was introduced to radio technology while serving in the army, and my mother worked in a civilian factory testing vacuum tubes. These experiences led them to pursue further education and finally embark on careers in engineering.

The G.I. Bill, signed by President Roosevelt in 1944, included financial support for veterans who wished to continue their education or technical training. Forty-nine percent of those admitted to college in 1947 were veterans. By 1956, nearly eight million World War II vets had taken advantage of G.I. Bill funding to advance their educations

Two of Dr. Bush's proposals had long-term positive effects on science. "As We May Think," an essay published in the *Atlantic Monthly* in 1945, laid out his vision for how machines might accelerate the development of human thought by giving people the ability to manage information efficiently. He outlined the design of a theoretical device called a Memex that would automatically keep track of a user's movements through a multimedia library, like a breadcrumb trail through a forest—or the bookmarks file of a modern Web browser. (The Memex later provided crucial inspiration for CERN researcher Tim Berners-Lee, the father of the World Wide Web.) Dr. Bush also produced a report called "Science—The Endless Frontier."

To make an impact, Dr. Bush's ideas needed some serious political clout behind them. He prevailed because he had the persistence of an eager entrepreneur in pursuit of backing for a new start-up. He convinced President Roosevelt to write a letter declaring that a national effort spearheaded by the Office of Scientific Research and Development, enlisting thousands of scientists in academia and private industry, "should be used in the days of peace ahead for the improvement of the national health, the creation of new enterprises bringing new jobs, and the betterment of the national standard of living."

Roosevelt challenged Dr. Bush to think big. "New frontiers of the mind are before us," he wrote from the White House, "and if they are pioneered with the same vision, boldness, and drive with which we have waged this war, we can create a fuller and more fruitful employment and a fuller and more fruitful life."

Dr. Bush's response, published in July 1945, was instrumental in setting a new tone for the nation, laying out a vision for collaboration between the government and the private sector to maximize the value that science and engineering could bring to the United States.

The themes of "The Endless Frontier" still hold true today: scientific progress is essential for the war against disease, our national security, and the public welfare; we must ensure a continuing supply of scientific talent; and research done during the war effort needs to be released to the public to be further advanced by industry and academia. His view that basic research should be recognized as its own discipline—funded separately from applied research and development—became a guiding principle of federal policy in the postwar era as new government agencies like NASA were created and existing ones grew.

The far-reaching R&D that resulted from the Manhattan Project was placed under the leadership of the Atomic Energy Commission in 1946. The National Institutes of Health expanded their support to nonfederal scientists, with a grant program that grew from approximately $4 million to over $100 million in a single decade. The NIH also broadened their scope to encompass new areas of medicine, including mental health and heart disease. The National Science Foundation was launched in 1950 to promote progress in all nonmedical areas of science and engineering by encouraging academic research and funding a wide range of individuals and institutions throughout the country.

Then, in October 1957, an ominous new star appeared in the skies over America, tracked by ham-radio buffs as it passed overhead: Sputnik 1, the first man-made object to orbit the Earth. "The Soviet Union had successfully launched a rocket with a satellite on board, and we couldn't do that," says Sally Ride, the country's first female astronaut and CEO of Sally Ride Science, which develops programs to inspire kids' interest in the subject. "Suddenly, we were no longer technologically superior. Everyone realized that if the Russians had rockets that could carry a satellite into orbit, they could also carry nuclear weapons to the United States. This deeply affected the psyche of the nation."

The American response was not merely to focus on building a bigger rocket. Instead, partly as a result of Dr. Bush's vision, the country responded to the broader challenge of increasing funding of research across a broad spectrum of fields. The excitement of the space race captured the imagination of a generation of young people, who went on to become leading scientists and engineers.

Congress demonstrated its commitment to increasing scientific and technical talent by passing the National Defense Education Act in 1958, investing in the future of the nation. The NDEA appropriated significant amounts of money for student loans, favoring the study of science, engineering, or foreign languages. It also provided funds to purchase equipment and finance National Defense Fellowships for graduate students.

In 1958, the Department of Defense established an Advanced Research Projects Agency to reestablish the nation's lead in military technology and avoid more surprises like Sputnik. ARPA's mission was to fund high-risk long-term research, focusing on large projects and systems. Later that year, President Eisenhower signed the National Aeronautics and Space Act, launching NASA. The stretch of Florida coastline between Miami and Jacksonville—the site of Cape Canaveral and the future Kennedy Space Center—became a hive of activity.

John F. Kennedy was elected to the White House in 1961. In a landmark speech before Congress in May of that year, he issued a stirring challenge: "First, I believe that this nation should commit itself to achieving the goal, before this decade is out, of landing a man on the moon and returning him safely to the Earth. No single space project in this period will be more impressive to mankind, or more important for the long-range exploration of space; and none will be so difficult or expensive to accomplish."

In response to a tragedy caused by the introduction of an inadequately tested drug called Thalidomide, the FDA was given more control over the approval of new pharmaceuticals. Prescribed to pregnant women for combating morning sickness, Thalidomide caused disabling birth defects in thousands of children. After the enactment of the Drug Efficacy Amendment in 1962, U.S. companies had to show that a new compound was both effective and safe. Regulations for clinical trials were tightened by adding requirements for informed consent and reporting of adverse effects.

This was an example of how the right type of regulation can help innovation. The FDA set standards so that doctors and patients were not afraid to try new drugs. "The Amendment said that if you are going to sell a drug in this country, you have to have scientific evidence demonstrated by adequate and well-controlled trials that the drug works," says former FDA commissioner David Kessler. "It was responsible for giving rise to the most competitive pharmaceutical industry in the world for several decades."

The country's leaders responded to world events with an appreciation of the role that science plays in society. They had vision, not just rhetoric, and they put actions behind their words to inspire and fund discovery. They understood that research was a necessity and not a luxury. The result was a foundation of research that was strong and wide. Federal support for R&D, as a percentage of GDP, almost tripled from 1953 to 1963. With complementary scopes and styles, the diverse funding agencies made possible a wide range of scientific exploration. They provided support primarily to research universities and big national and independent laboratories like SRI, and also to corporations.

In the technology industry, several companies that were either monopolies or dominant players in their industries had the profit margins and vision to invest in a broad range of research. AT&T Bell Labs, RCA Sarnoff Labs, IBM Research, and Xerox PARC—in league with academic institutions—all made huge advances in computing, physics, communications, electronics, and other areas of science. Their parent companies did not expect to see short-term financial gains from the work at these labs.

In some cases, they saw returns from sources that they might not have expected. "If you look at the return to Xerox solely on the laser printing business, it more than pays back their entire investment in PARC," says former PARC researcher John Shoch, who became president of Xerox's office systems division. The benefits of this research—from the transistor, to lasers, to the

Internet—extended to all areas of American society and the global economy.

We can learn a lot about innovation from institutions like PARC, Bell Labs, and ARPA. They had different approaches and cultures, but their successes illustrate the incredible potential of having the right combination of leadership, resources, vision, talent, and trust.

AUGMENTING HUMAN INTELLECT

ARPA's leadership carried forward several of the philosophies that Dr. Bush had advanced so effectively during the war. The agency was committed to funding high-risk research and enlisting the brightest civilian engineers and scientists while maintaining minimum bureaucratic overhead. By the early 1960s, computing and communications were playing ever-increasing roles in military technology, and ARPA created its Information Processing Techniques Office (IPTO) to focus on research in these emerging fields. The first director of IPTO was J. C. R. Licklider, a soft-spoken visionary with degrees in physics, math, and psychology.

Like Dr. Bush before him, Licklider believed that computers would someday be used as tools for augmenting thought and creativity—a view that he laid out in a prescient paper called "Man-Computer Symbiosis." IPTO directors held their positions for two years, and as each handpicked his successor, "Lick's" vision of open-ended inquiry was maintained and expanded. After their term, these directors would go back into research or industry, inspiring students and employees to carry on the mission.

Whether you're reading your e-mail, opening up a spreadsheet, typing a memo, paying your bills online, or just surfing the Web, you're relying on a graphical user interface and local and global networking schemes based on IPTO-funded work carried out in the 1960s and 1970s. In this golden age of ARPA-sponsored research, universities and corporate labs teamed up to perform breakthrough experiments as scientists and engineers created the powerful new digital tools that we now take for granted. New bit-mapped displays made onscreen graphics and digital typography possible, and smiley faces were transformed from :-) to ☺. With the addition of a device that enabled you to navigate in this new virtual space—a mouse—the "point-and-click" interface that is universal in personal computing today was born.

Paul Baran was a young researcher at Rand when the U.S. Defense Department realized that its strategic command-and-control systems were vulnerable because they were over-centralized. By studying the ways in which the neural networks in the human brain recover from a catastrophic injury like a stroke, Baran and his team conceptualized models for a new kind of telecommunications network that would resemble a fishnet, with redundant links that enabled the network to automatically route communications around damaged areas.

They discovered that when you have three times as many links as you need, there would always be a viable path through the network. "We found that a certain magical property popped up," Baran recalls. "But we didn't know how to build such networks, because the digital technology required was just coming out of the lab." He and his colleagues set out to construct a digital command-and-control network that would be able to survive a nuclear attack. The result was the packet-switching technology that is fundamental to the way the Internet works.

Alan Kay, one of the architects of the graphical user interface, has always been guided by his belief that the best way to predict the future is to invent it. His passion for making computers more accessible to everyone was contagious as we talked for several hours about the golden days of ARPA. "My impression of the ARPA community when I joined it as a grad student in the 1960s was of 'the ARPA dream'—that the eventual destiny of computing was to create a global network that would work as an intellectual amplifier for everyone. I do not believe we would have gotten there if Licklider hadn't been there at the beginning," he says.

The IPTO leaders shared not only a vision of how computers could enhance our lives, but also a set of beliefs as to how government funding could best be applied to encourage radical change, rather than just incremental improvement. They believed that it was their job to be stewards of innovation and enablers of genius by framing the big picture and outlining the challenges we face as a society. But they did not try to force specific goals or theories on the groups they funded. ARPA identified centers of excellence at specific universities and labs without concern for geographic distribution, and funded teams of scientists with diverse backgrounds. It granted multiyear contracts with very broad scope, allowing graduate students to rely on funding through their Ph.D. years. This allowed them to achieve the critical mass and stability of funding required for significant research advances.

As a graduate student at UCLA, Vint Cerf participated in the development of ARPANET, and, as a Stanford professor, he played a leadership role in the creation of the Internet. "The graduate students were given enormous latitude by the principal investigators to go off and tackle problems," he recalls. "ARPA had the ability to essentially decide who was going to do what with relative freedom. They took a problem and went around to the smartest people they could find, asking them, 'How can you solve this?' Then they paid them to do it."

One of the teams funded by ARPA was Doug Engelbart's Augmentation Research Center at SRI. Engelbart is best known as the inventor of the computer mouse, but his contributions were much broader. Inspired by Dr. Bush's "As We May Think," Engelbart's lab created prototypes for word processing, the storage and retrieval of electronic documents, hypertext, windowed interfaces, e-mail, and video teleconferencing—all in the 1960s.

Seeing a video of Engelbart's famous demo of these technologies is like watching an old black-and-white science fiction movie in which the technology looks a bit clunky but offers a prescient foretaste of the future. You can't help be amazed at how much these concepts, introduced to the world in 1968, influenced the computing environments we use today.

Openness and collaboration were two of ARPA's key goals, and barriers were actively eliminated. Innovation was encouraged in an atmosphere of trust. The agency hired good people and told them to find other people they trusted to get the job done. Technically savvy program managers were given the freedom and resources to shape multiple contracts and stimulate new areas of exploration.

Proposals did not have to go through a long peer review process. Researchers spent their time working, rather than grinding out lengthy funding requests. "We could write our proposals on half a page, because they were really just goals," says Alan Kay. "We needed to invent a scalable network—what else can you say? We used to say that ARPA is vision rather than goals, and people rather than projects."

ARPA brought researchers together to form communities by leveraging the nascent network and sponsoring meetings between principal investigators and graduate students. Xerox PARC did contract work for ARPA so that it could attract top Ph.D. students who had worked on ARPA-funded projects and wanted to stay connected. "The people recruited to PARC were those who believed in this dream, and were nutty enough to not be doctrinaire about how they were going to go about doing it. Xerox PARC could only have happened because of ARPA," says Kay. This kind of community building turned out to be key in advancing the state of personal computing. Because Xerox's monopoly on copiers was wildly profitable, PARC had the resources and the expertise to prototype the large numbers of systems necessary to experiment with network computing environments.

"ARPA was a magical entity," recalls Bob Metcalfe, now a general partner at Polaris Venture Partners. The legacy of its leaders and researchers goes beyond their technological contributions to include the multitude of professors, graduate students, researchers, and developers whose lives and careers they influenced—directly and indirectly—for decades.

THE REACH OF BELL LABS

It's hard to believe that the transistor, the cell phone, the laser, the light-emitting diode, the Unix operating system, digital camera chips, and six Nobel Prizes all came out of the same lab—and a corporate one at that. But they did. In its most prolific years—between 1960 and 1983—Bell Labs employed approximately 25,000 people, most of whom were focused on creating technology for improved telephone service. But more than a thousand of those scientists and engineers were focused on very basic research in a broad range of scientific fields, including physics, chemistry, and computer science. The organization was unique in that its parent company, AT&T, was a government-sponsored monopoly, and its financing came from a tax on phone service.

In the early days, the company was completely vertically integrated. Bell built everything itself, from handsets to switching systems. It not only pioneered the use of microwave radio, but grew its own crystals for the quartz plates required to build the oscillators that made those radios work. Thus, Bell Labs was able to attract the best scientists and engineers from a wide variety of disciplines. It hired 10 percent of the electrical engineering Ph.D.s in the country every year. For many young scientists and engineers, Bell Labs was the ideal place to start their careers. Whether they chose to stay in that environment, move to academia, or move on to industry, Bell Labs provided a great training ground for a generation of innovators. "The best thing about the old Bell Labs was that there was a world expert in every subject of interest, and that expert would be right down the hall," says Robert Lucky, who went to work there as a new Ph.D. in 1962.

There was a built-in channel for Bell Labs technology: the company would just go to the local telephone companies and tell them what they would be buying. The scientists were driven by the needs that they saw around them. AT&T was spending $80 million a year replacing vacuum tubes, so the research director decided to launch an effort to replace them. Wartime development work on radar had led to advances in the field of semiconductors, and a Bell Labs researcher named Bill Shockley put together a team to see how these new materials might be applied to replacing tube-based switches. In 1948, the *New York Times* announced the discovery of the transistor . . . on page 46. No one imagined that one day, a single silicon chip would contain over a billion transistors, and that this humble discovery would become the building block of the computer industry and a whole new world of electronic devices.

Large organizations like AT&T rarely manage to be so innovative. Bell Labs had many levels of hierarchy, but at the bottom were teams composed of a dozen or so scientists and engineers who worked on whatever they wanted. The department heads did not micromanage the researchers; instead, they oversaw the development of a portfolio of projects. "In my career as a member of the technical staff at Bell Labs, no one ever gave me an explicit assignment," says Lucky. "The competition came, not from commercial pressures, but from the scientific acclaim that could be had. It was assumed that you were self-motivated and self-led, and if you didn't succeed in this context, you found a different job."

Bell Labs had leadership with a long-term outlook and a stable funding environment that did not depend on company profits. A critical mass of scientists from a variety of disciplines was given the freedom to explore and brought its efforts to bear on solving real-world problems.

ENTREPRENEURIAL ENGINEERS

The strong tradition of research established by ARPA and Bell Labs provided a foundation for what would become a critical source of innovation in the years to come: the start-up company. From the 1950s on, entrepreneurialism began to play an increasingly important role in computing, communications, and biotech.

Recognizing the transistor's broad potential, Bill Shockley left Bell Labs and headed west. In 1956, he launched Shockley Semiconductor near the Stanford campus in Palo Alto. Fred Terman, the university's provost and dean of engineering, was an early supporter of collaboration between academia and industry. Palo Alto had already become a hot spot for radio and military electronics development. Companies like Varian and Hewlett-Packard attracted top talent, offering benefits like profit sharing and establishing a precedent for the culture of Silicon Valley as an innovation incubator.

As start-ups grew, forward-looking employees would often leave to launch companies of their own. One of Shockley's first hires was Robert Noyce, who had become fascinated by transistors at college. A year after joining the company, Noyce led an exodus of scientists—known in Valley lore as the "traitorous eight"—who were upset over Shockley's management style. With financing from the pioneering venture capitalist Arthur Rock, Fairchild Semiconductor was born in 1957, establishing a pattern of engineers becoming entrepreneurs.

Congress passed the Small Business Investment Act in 1958, and innovative financial professionals and ex-entrepreneurs teamed up to launch the first venture capital (VC) partnerships. Arthur Rock left banking to focus on VC in 1961. Eugene Kleiner, one of the scientists who left Shockley, cofounded Kleiner Perkins in 1972. Thirty new venture firms were created between 1968 and 1975.

Eleven years after the founding of Fairchild Semiconductor, Noyce and Gordon Moore, believing that they could achieve more on their own, left to start Intel. Joining them was Andy Grove, who would later become Intel's CEO and one of the country's leading executives. With a culture that embraced innovation's core values and proximity to two great research universities—UC Berkeley and Stanford—the Valley was quickly filled with small, specialized companies that collaborated and competed to create new industries.

The successful venture capitalists of the time had a philosophy similar to ARPA's, with a different time horizon. They funded great people, took risks, did not require fully developed concepts or markets before investment, and knew that new ventures rarely end up looking like their original business plans. They were willing to bank on intuition and trust, combining patience with an understanding that it might take five to seven years for them to see a return. This encouragement of risk—along with an acceptance of failure—was what made the Valley unique.

A commitment to long-term, high-risk research by government and industry led to discoveries that inspired innovation for decades. ARPA funding led to the Internet and the Web. Without Bell Labs, we would not have PCs or cell phones. NASA research yielded fruits far beyond space exploration. Technology first developed for Earth remote-sensing satellites is used today in cardiac imaging systems. Black & Decker's Dust Buster evolved from devices that the company developed to enable Apollo astronauts to gather rock and soil samples from the moon's surface.

The addition to industry of venture-backed start-ups brought new levels of risk, as many start-up companies failed. But the successes drove significantly more reward as fresh companies translated new ideas into products and profits. Start-ups became a driving force for innovation. But soon, increased competition—in part created by these new companies—was to have an impact on larger corporations. In addition, the government's incentives for funding longer-term research started to change. The balance of the Innovation Ecosystem was about to shift, testing the strength of its foundation.

CHAPTER 4

NARROWING HORIZONS

By the 1970s, as a result of the government's deep commitment to science and the emergence of the start-up economy, America had reestablished its technological preeminence. This leadership position benefited national security and spurred economic growth. But intensified global competition and increasing pressures from Wall Street led large companies to focus on efficiency and cut back on research.

Support for start-up companies remained strong, with entrepreneurs, venture capitalists, customers, and the economy all reaping benefits. These new small companies, however, needed to be more focused and could not conduct the broader exploratory work of the corporate labs.

As the motivations driving government funding and policy started to change, innovations continued to stream out of the research community, but many of them reflected more of a focus on applied research than on the kind of basic, open-ended exploration that distinguished Vannevar Bush's vision of an "endless frontier."

In the 1970s, for the first time, industry's investment in R&D surpassed that of the federal government. This trend was a positive indication that industry was growing and investing. But with it came a shift of funding from research toward development, and a narrowing of the overall horizon. The incentives to continue planting the seeds necessary for long-term, sustainable innovation were no longer aligned.

The Mansfield Amendment, passed by Congress in 1973, limited appropriations for defense research through ARPA to technologies with direct military applications. This new policy reduced funding for some of the life-changing initiatives that ARPA had supported and sent a signal to researchers that more changes were coming. ARPA was renamed DARPA to reinforce its affiliation with defense.

The new legislation changed the way in which funds were granted, which can be even more important than the overall number of dollars. Pixar founder Ed Catmull, who did research at the University of Utah in the 1970s, felt the pain of this shift: "I remember ARPA saying very explicitly near the end of their support for computer graphics, 'Our part is done.' The mindset was that the work had been seeded and that industry should now take over. They didn't think of their responsibility as, 'Good, let's keep seeding more things.'"

The Vietnam War diverted money from basic research and resulted in increasing resistance to the military among university scientists. The Internet research that Vint Cerf was leading at Stanford continued to get full support from the government, because it was easy to explain to DARPA how a communication system capable of surviving a nuclear war could serve the needs of the military. But Cerf also had to make the people who were doing the research comfortable with their sponsors. "I found myself trying to figure out what kind of civilian problems could be solved using our research," he says. He specifically avoided the use of military terms when describing problems to researchers, while ensuring that their work was relevant to military needs.

Government budgets were tightening overall, and DARPA contracts were becoming more directed. As the information technology and biotech industries showed promise, funding was directed toward these areas, at the expense of continuing to fuel basic research in the physical and environmental sciences.

ENTREPRENEURIAL INNOVATION TAKES OFF

The oil crisis in the early 1970s had a chilling effect on the U.S. economy, putting pressure on big companies and individuals throughout the world, but the scrappy little start-ups kept coming. The founding of Nasdaq opened up another avenue of financial return, which in turn spurred more entrepreneurial activity. Unlike the NYSE's, Nasdaq's "trading floor" existed only in cyberspace. Nasdaq had lower listing requirements and fees, creating a vehicle that enabled smaller, more volatile companies to access public markets and fund their future growth.

Legislation allowing pension funds to invest in venture capital firms significantly increased the dollars available for start-ups. The incentives of entrepreneurs, venture capitalists, the public capital markets, and customers were all aligned to create companies that made money for their investors. From the entrepreneur's perspective, these companies existed to develop a new technology, drug, vaccine, or device that could change the world.

The important new field of molecular biology was launched with the discovery of recombinant DNA in the early 1970s by Herbert Boyer, a biochemist at UC San Francisco, and associate professor of medicine Stanley Cohen at Stanford. The promise of revolutionizing medicine, coupled with the stock market's appetite for risk, created an environment in which a lot of the early research was done by industry, funded by venture capitalists and the public markets.

Genentech, founded by Boyer and venture capitalist Robert Swanson in 1976, became the poster child for the biotech industry. Smart scientists were given the tools, funding, and autonomy to ask the big questions, restoring serendipity as a potential source of significant value. "Genentech was light-years ahead of everybody else in molecular biology. The super-geek biologists who worked there were the best in the world," explains Larry Lasky, an early fellow at the company. "We had three things lacking in academia—money, freedom, and technology." Within its first four years, the company had cloned both human insulin and human growth hormone and went public, raising $35 million before generating any significant revenues or profit.

The promise of working with the best of the best took precedence over the safety of enlisting at a large corporation with a known brand. When I graduated from Stanford in 1976, I interviewed at all of the established computer companies—Hewlett-Packard, Xerox, and Intel—as well as at a new 50-person company called Zilog that had been launched by former Intel employees. I chose to work at Zilog because a friend of my parents said that the smartest people he knew worked there. Many of my friends thought I was crazy to join such a small company. I didn't even know what a stock option was. My motivation was the potential to make an impact in this new phase of the computer industry. Zilog was a hotbed of innovation that exposed me to the excitement of start-up life.

The PC on your desk, the video game your kids are playing in the next room, and the PDA in your pocket all had their origins at bold start-ups of the 1970s like Apple, Microsoft, and Atari. There was nowhere more exciting to be than Silicon Valley.

SERVING TWO MASTERS

Economic factors exerted increasing pressure on government policy in the 1980s. The Reagan administration's crusade to reduce the size of government resulted in changes in federal funding and procurement, which further shortened research time frames. New guidelines stipulated that the government should not undertake any projects that could be done by industry, and projects that were funded were directed to pursue solutions compatible with both government and industry— so-called dual-use technologies. A prospective technology designed to provide benefits for enterprise data-center environments also needed to work for an army field deployment.

Ambitious system projects like ARPANET continued to get support. The NSF funded a series of supercomputer centers, linked by a high-speed network that became a key building block of the Internet. But the basic science that led to the creation of these networks in the first place was no longer a priority.

People who had been looking forward five to ten years were now looking only two to three years out, because they had to show commercial justification for their work. "I saw this huge retraction in the research horizon," recalls Van Jacobson, who was at Lawrence Berkeley Labs and is now a research fellow at PARC. "In Washington, you had to demonstrate two things: you had to use commercial gear wherever possible, and whatever you were doing had to be commercially relevant." The concept of developing technologies that would be useful for both government and industry sounds good, but it limited broad exploration. And in this case, smaller government did not result in either more innovation or greater efficiency.

Changes in university licensing policies had unintended consequences for innovation. In 1980, Congress passed the Bayh-Dole Act, giving universities ownership of intellectual property resulting from federally funded research. The universities now had the responsibility, as stewards of their discoveries, to see that those discoveries benefited society. Technology transfer offices were created to move ideas from campus labs out to the commercial world, where increasing numbers of entrepreneurs were waiting to capitalize on them.

But there was a difference between the intent and the outcome of Bayh-Dole. As these licensing offices grew in size and power, at some universities they became viewed as a new source of revenue, which encouraged researchers to emphasize short-term applied research that could be licensed more quickly.

"It has made me very nervous to think that universities themselves are becoming motivated by capitalizing on their research properties, as opposed to allowing the research to be motivated by the desire to know and to share," says Internet pioneer Vint Cerf. The pace of research accelerates remarkably when there is adequate sharing going on, which is what publication is all about. The Human Genome Database is just one example of how progress can move forward more quickly when sharing of data is required.

Bayh-Dole created a conflict between scientific motivations and financial ones—between figuring out how to capitalize on intellectual property and the information sharing that is the coin of the realm in academia. As computer networking took off in the mid-1980s, people became less willing to share the fruits of their research. "If you were to try to do today what ARPA did in the 1960s and 1970s," says Cerf, "it might not work, because of the commercial interest of people who want to turn their ideas into money." Similar anxiety about intellectual property rights began to reshape biomedical research, resulting in the patenting of genes.

"The notion of the separation of academe went away," observes *New York Times* writer John Markoff, who has tracked technology and Silicon Valley since the early 1980s. "Before, there was a community of researchers who were not entrepreneurial. There was a bright line, and you kept your work pure by not making it a business enterprise." This shift was heralded by some as progress: academic researchers were being brought down from their ivory towers to face real-world problems. But the effect was to narrow the scope of research to work that could be ported to the marketplace as quickly as possible.

Faculty and students who felt inspired to be entrepreneurs naturally took that path. But pushing researchers to become entrepreneurs often backfired, resulting in failed companies and little research of importance. Although most universities were far more successful raising money from successful alumni than from the returns on any one piece of intellectual property, licensing offices continued to grow in influence.

University research was not the only victim of this push toward commercialization. As the marketplace became increasingly competitive, corporations with their own labs could no longer sustain the long view. Organizations like Bell Labs were redeployed to focus on the development of advanced technology that could more directly affect business results. An antitrust suit by the U.S. Justice Department forced AT&T to spin off the Baby Bells, and with this split went part of Bell Labs. The previously renowned research center became leaner and more consumer-focused. The days of broad scientific exploration were over.

OPTIMIZING FOR EFFICIENCY

Businesses, facing intense competition at home and from abroad, became obsessed with maximizing their profit margins. The most admired corporate executives in the 1980s were those who championed greater efficiency, higher productivity, and a strong customer focus. Supply chain management and just-in-time inventory were a key part of the change.

A new management technique called Six Sigma—a highly disciplined methodology for eliminating defects through precise measurement and control—was hailed as the way to improve quality levels in manufacturing. Advances in IT provided instantaneous access to detailed information about all aspects of business, enabling leaders to drive short-term incremental innovation in their internal processes—and in their products. The role of chief information officer was elevated as companies recognized the importance of having access to up-to-the-minute data. IT suddenly got the attention of top management and boards of directors, and technology acquisitions became a subject of executive cocktail-party conversation.

But many companies offering products based on science or technology were now being run by professional managers with legal, financial, or sales backgrounds who had little understanding of, or respect for, science itself. Efficiency also reigned supreme on Wall Street, as companies sought to produce more predictable results. If you beat analysts' estimates by a penny, you were lauded, but if you were a penny below, you were crushed.

As companies looked for ways to manage costs, health care became a primary target. Employer-sponsored health insurance was getting more and more expensive, and companies switched to plans that limited the employees' choice of providers and treatment options. Though this contained costs for a period, the draconian approaches used by managed-care organizations undercut the popularity of their plans, and these savings were short-lived. Many of these organizations replaced a physician's commitment to a standard of care with administrative decision making.

There were many hidden costs of the focus on short-term efficiency. Organizations lost their tolerance for anything that couldn't be managed through the metrics dashboard on the executive's desktop PC. Innovation can be a messy and inefficient process; it's not one that can be managed through simple metrics.

It's hard to think broadly and go beyond incremental improvements when the mantra of the organization is *focus, focus, focus.* "The very process of a company becoming good at its business is often a process of driving out the unknowns and the uncertainties," says Applied Minds cofounder Danny Hillis. "Lots of people have gotten much better at getting the slop out of the system. Unfortunately, that slop was where a lot of the innovation was happening. It provided the openness to look for new opportunities."

IT AND BIOTECH DRIVE THE MARKET

From the perspective of Silicon Valley, the 1980s were incredible. Young companies like Apple, Genentech, and Microsoft were going public, and people started to make real money. Investment banks that had historically talked only to major corporations targeted small IT and life sciences companies as growth markets. Dollars poured into venture funds with partners who understood the role that risk plays in generating returns.

In 1981, inspired by our experience at Zilog, Bill Carrico and I decided to launch Bridge Communications, one of the original companies in the nascent networking market. Our products were to be built around Ethernet, a technology that was not yet the standard, or even a recognized winner. A week before we were to close our first round of funding, a market research firm declared that Ethernet was not going to make it, and that a competing technology, developed by Wang, would become the standard. Bill was 31 years old and I was 26. We didn't have a lot of experience, but we had vision and conviction. We believed that Ethernet was going to be around for the long haul. Our investors—who understood little about the technology issues—believed in us, took a risk, and wrote the check. They gave us the opportunity to pursue our dream. Ethernet became the international standard, and Wang is now defunct. Bridge was financially successful, and the risk paid off.

Start-ups became the research engines of the pharmaceutical industry. "When I started doing biotech investments, all we did was research," says Sam Colella, managing director at Versant Ventures. "There weren't any products. Companies were started by venture, and then a large amount of money came from the federal government and business partners."

As more technology and biotech companies went public, a group of savvy analysts emerged to help investors understand these esoteric companies and products. Though many companies ended up being acquired, the goal of most entrepreneurs was to build a company for the long term, and access to the public markets enabled them to realize that dream. I still remember the excitement—tempered by a sense of responsibility—the morning in 1985 when Bridge Communications began trading as a public company.

Customers in the application community with the capacity for change greeted the new generation of start-ups with open arms. The development of new materials, products, drugs, and medical procedures was welcomed by enterprises, consumers, and the medical world, all of which were eager to try new things. Companies looked to new computing solutions and software to help them compete by increasing productivity, lowering costs, and reaching out to their customers in new ways. They were willing to put their trust in a small, unknown company with a great idea.

As computing and communications technology advanced, its influence grew beyond the normal force of innovation driving innovation. Electronic mail and the sharing of computing resources over the Internet enhanced the collaborative process in all communities of the Ecosystem, enabling people to capitalize on one another's work and allowing businesses to collect feedback from their employees, customers, and partners throughout the world.

The World Wide Web increased the availability of information about all fields of science. The ability to learn about new advances in any field, happening anywhere in the world, became limited only by one's own curiosity and time. Beyond the benefits of collaboration, the availability of cost-effective, high-performance processing and high-capacity data storage accelerated experimentation and analysis.

New ways of using computers emerged to test concepts and products from silicon chips to clothing and cars. Dramatic declines in the cost of storage and processing enabled a new level of data warehousing and mining, making it possible for companies like Amazon to offer product selections based on previous buying patterns, or advertisers to target specific demographics more accurately.

The discovery of DNA in the 1950s occurred at about the same time as the discovery of the semiconductor. But there was no way that scientists could deal with the vast number of variables and complexity of genetics without the aid of computers. It took decades for computers to reach the level of performance needed to be useful in advancing the field. "It was almost like there was a holdup in biology until the semiconductor led to the type of computing power that allowed you to be able to look at a system that had 20,000 independent variables, or genes," says Genomic Health CEO Randy Scott. "But once the technology for experimentation started to come into play and the computer technology was there to be able to analyze it, that's when the game really started."

The 1980s were a time of growth and increasing potential, as information technology reduced barriers to innovation by providing more processing power for experimentation and better communications among scientists, engineers, and business-people. But there were dark clouds gathering on the horizon that few people could see in a time of increasing prosperity.

LOSING OUR LEAD

With the fall of the Berlin Wall in 1989 and the demise of the Soviet Union, defense budgets began a steady decline, and there was continued focus on reducing the federal deficit. Pressure on research funding increased overall. The technology industry was so strong that no one noticed that we had stopped planting the seeds of future growth. The rest of the world was not standing still. The number of articles in science and engineering published by U.S. authors stayed flat through the 1990s, while people in other nations were growing more prolific.

As our research base quietly eroded, other forces started conspiring to take their toll on America's innovative momentum. Large corporations were looking for ways to compete more effectively as their costs for health care, litigation, and marketing increased. The continued focus on efficiency led to an increase in mergers. As pharmaceutical companies got larger, management shifted resources from innovation in science to innovation in salesmanship, marketing drugs directly to doctors and potential consumers.

"Look at the story of Genentech and look at the story of Pfizer," says former FDA commissioner David Kessler. "Over the last several decades, Genentech has believed that the only thing important to its long-term success is its R&D, its ability to discover new molecules. Everything is science-based. It's willing to look at hard diseases and smaller markets, areas where there is greatest need, and take risks to develop drugs where no one else is. After absorbing multiple companies, Pfizer, on the other hand, has become so big, its strategy is to move away from

R&D, toward marketing and promotion, and become a wellness lifestyle company. They have moved away from the science."

The pharmaceutical industry focused on making drugs for which millions of prescriptions are written every year. "We drove the world to a blockbuster model," says Genomic Health CEO Randy Scott. "It has become so expensive to develop a drug that the only drugs you can justify developing have to be worth half a billion to a billion dollars or more."

To sell those drugs, Big Pharma pushed for the ability to market its products directly to consumers. "I opposed it for seven years while I was at the FDA," says David Kessler. "I basically put my body on the line and said no, because if you're really focused on the science, and your product works, you can get the word out to those who need it. You don't need the hype." Kessler left the agency in 1997, and within weeks, the FDA changed its policy. Dollars spent on pharmaceutical advertising have increased 28 percent a year since then. Some of the money spent on innovation in marketing would have been better spent on researching technologies to allow us to discover and develop drugs at a lower cost.

Innovation in health care has been further hampered by the increasing threat of malpractice suits and the rising costs of insurance premiums for doctors. Malpractice suits can be viewed as a roundabout way of ensuring better care, but they are often abused, creating preemptive behavior on the part of physicians that can lead to unnecessary tests, higher costs, and even additional health risks. "The effect is so insidious that it's become hard to distinguish *good* medicine from *defensive* medicine," says Mark Josephs, emergency department director at Exeter Hospital in New Hampshire. "In the emergency department, we might perform a costly cervical-spine CAT scan in order to rule out the minuscule chance of a fracture. The scan exposes you to some chance of getting thyroid cancer much further down the road. The emergency MD would not be held responsible for that cancer, but will be sued if a fracture is missed." These kinds of trade-offs are made every day as doctors and hospitals try to practice good medicine while watching their backs.

As companies with fluctuating earnings cycles went public, class-action securities litigation became more commonplace. A Supreme Court ruling that eased the plaintiff's burden of proof led to the formation of larger plaintiff classes and larger awards and damages. Like overreaching malpractice suits, frivolous business lawsuits became more common, taking additional management focus and funding away from innovation and reducing the appetite for risk. Some relief came with reform legislation later in the decade, but the abuse of security and employee litigation grew, with significant dollars going to insurance premiums and lawyers' fees.

America's Innovation Ecosystem was already beginning its decline, but this was mostly invisible because we were on the threshold of an explosion of new technologies, companies, and sudden wealth that *Wired* magazine founder Louis Rossetto described as a "Digital Revolution . . . whipping through our lives like a Bengali typhoon." By the time the typhoon had blown over, the foundations of the Ecosystem had been weakened. But to the young people who started flocking to Silicon Valley in the mid-1990s, it looked as if the party was just getting started.

ACCELERATING OUT OF CONTROL

One of the most important research developments of the decade came from outside the United States. Tim Berners-Lee, a researcher at CERN in Switzerland, developed a new way of displaying and transmitting documents on the Net, inspired in part by concepts demonstrated in Doug Engelbart's demo. He christened this new technology the World Wide Web, and it created a new way of sharing information that would go far beyond his expectations of improving communication among the physicists at CERN.

Marc Andreessen, the future cofounder of Netscape, was inspired by Berners-Lee's research, but found his initial software implementations primitive and hard to use. At the time, Andreessen was an undergraduate student working part-time at the University of Illinois. Starting in October 1992, he and a small team of programmers dedicated their nights and weekends to prototyping a universal client for the Internet, including a graphical front end for the Web. Within three months, they distributed an early version of Mosaic. What started as a side project grew quickly. Andreessen was able to leverage decades of prior work by researchers in the fields of networking and graphical user interfaces. "The way I look at it, Mosaic was the final layer of frosting on this cake that was baked by others for 30 years," Andreessen says. "It spread virally." By April there were tens of thousands of users, and at the end of 1993 there were at least a million users.

Then in 1995, Netscape went public. Why did the stock market value a company that was a little over a year old at over a billion dollars? "The Netscape browser had become a phenomenon, especially among college-age techie types," says Peter Currie, Netscape's former chief financial officer and now president of Currie Capital. "Everyone who used it thought, 'How fun. I'll buy a piece of this company'—including people who had never bought a share of stock before." They rang up brokers throughout the country and put in orders to buy Netscape shares when they became available.

Most investors put an upper limit on what they're willing to pay when they place an order. But the new crop of 20- to 30-

year-olds—who understood the digital revolution better than they did the stock market—did not. Netscape's investment banker, Morgan Stanley, even had to put in a dedicated fax line just for people requesting a copy of the Netscape prospectus. When the stock was supposed to begin trading, there were all of these orders to buy, but no one wanted to sell. A stock that was supposed to start trading at $28 a share opened in the $70s. Larger investors who had passed up opportunities to get in early with shares of Apple, Genentech, or Microsoft sensed something big and jumped in. The financial world was experiencing the first signs of the potential impact of individuals empowered by the Internet. The craziness that is now called "the dot-com bubble" had begun.

By then, the role of start-ups in driving innovation was becoming so clear that many larger companies were beginning to depend on them for their own growth. Partnerships and acquisitions became a key strategy for "outsourcing" innovation as companies in the technology and biotech industries raced to keep up. But as we moved faster and faster, time horizons got shorter and shorter. This was true for start-ups as well, as companies were created and funded specifically for a quick return by being bought out by a larger company. Many networking companies were funded with the hope of being acquired by Cisco, which had more than 30,000 employees by the end of the decade.

Every entrepreneur, VC, investment banker, and public investor wanted to be part of the next Netscape. Venture funds raced for the hottest deals, taking too much risk based on too little data. The focus shifted from traditional business measures, such as revenue and earnings, to trendy metrics borrowed from the entertainment industry, such as the number of "eyeballs" attracted to a Web site. In the coding language of the Web, URL means *universal resource locator*—a pointer to a site's network address. In the heady atmosphere of the late 1990s, Eric Schmidt, who was then Sun's CTO, said to me with a smile, "You know what URL stands for? Ubiquity now, revenue later."

This was an accurate description of the business model of the so-called new economy. New companies forgot their business fundamentals. I remember talking to a friend in early 2000 about his niece, who had just joined a dot-com whose business model she described as "raising money." These companies, founded to get a piece of the Internet land grab, saw their role as collecting cash to attract as much attention as possible. They didn't have any clear plans for how they would become profitable.

The Internet itself suddenly became a type of business. People didn't stop to think that this was the equivalent of suggesting that if a company relied on the telephone to do business, that made it a "phone company." The pace moved from fast to frenetic, and first movers (theoretically) had the advantage.

We were shifting from an economy based on manufacturing and distribution to one driven by information. When I was Cisco's CTO, every day another large, mature company would come to the customer center to learn how to best leverage the Internet and accommodate the change.

Stock market growth crossed the line from strong to irrational exuberance. Money poured into mutual funds that were competing for investors' dollars by demonstrating quarter-to-quarter performance; this translated into more pressure to favor short-term results over long-term health.

Journalism became more competitive and sensational as the 24-hour news cycle came to dominate both TV and the Web. CNBC and its competitors covered the market from sunrise to sundown, providing information and opinions to a broader set of investors than ever before. Day trading became a profession, and suddenly students, those who worked at home, and unemployed people all over the world were logging on to sites like E*TRADE, chasing the dream of becoming instant millionaires with a few clicks of the mouse.

The ubiquity of PCs and the Internet made it too easy for these investors to become reckless gamblers. "People no longer had to call some broker and say, 'I'd like to buy Digital Data Whack,'" says David Liddle, general partner at U.S. Venture Partners. "In the past, that broker would have told them, 'Well, I don't know; let me see what the analysts say; it doesn't really fit your risk profile.' There was none of that friction."

Suddenly financial analysts and reporters were TV stars. Instead of observing and analyzing trends to help sophisticated investors, they were talking to less experienced retail investors through the media, often influencing the stocks directly and creating a new level of volatility. More and more dollars were being invested based on less and less understanding.

Airline attendants and orthodontists were suddenly paying $100 a share for stock in companies that didn't yet have any products. "Greed was clearly a major driver," recalls Hossein Eslambolchi, who was CTO of AT&T. "People were chasing very quick money." The SEC investigated a 15-year-old high school student for stock market fraud. The teenager had made up to $74,000 a day trading stocks from his bedroom in a New Jersey suburb.

There was plenty of innovation at the surface, with a flood of new companies touting "revolutionary" business models. The industry was growing so fast that it was hard to catch one's breath. The momentum of the high-tech industry was out of control in a way that would backfire on science and technology innovation.

I'll never forget the day I told our employees at Precept that we had just sold the company to Cisco for $82 million—a good price indeed for a company with $1 million in revenue. One of our engineers came into my office upset, telling me that I had sold way too low, too soon. "I expected to make at least a million dollars when I came here," he said. Little did we know that Cisco's stock was about to increase fivefold, with the company reaching a $500 billion market cap at the peak of the bubble.

The tech world had certainly changed—a sense of entitlement had set in. "Turnover was so high that any concept of loyalty went out the window," recalls Marc Andreessen. "There I was dealing with day-to-day management issues, knowing there was a 50 percent chance that the person I was dealing with was going to bail in three months." The tech industry as a whole became much more mercenary, and people who wanted to patiently build a company—and a culture—became rare exceptions. "In that crazy period, you saw the emergence of the entrepreneurial equivalent of the day trader," recalls Heidi Roizen, a venture capitalist who is now CEO of SkinnySongs. "They saw an opportunity to get rich by building something that somebody wanted to buy and flipping it."

Innovation and entrepreneurialism are closely linked, but they are not always aligned. Most entrepreneurs are motivated by a commitment both to their vision and to the promise of making money. But entrepreneurs who previously focused on building great products and changing the world were instead tracking their stock growth minute to minute on TV monitors tuned to CNBC in the company lobby.

During the bubble's expansion, our focus shifted to instant gratification, and entrepreneurship came to be at odds with innovation. We lost our patience, and with it our ability or willingness to take the time to ask questions. This dynamic spread beyond investment strategies to people's expectations in other realms. Patients increasingly wanted their health care to be as quick and action-oriented as the rest of their lives, demanding a pill or a test that they had heard about on TV or over the Internet.

The speed at which everything was moving affected not just people's time horizon, but also the depth of their insight. We created a generation of PowerPoint addicts who spend their time creating bullet points, animations, and graphics to dazzle their audience, instead of providing thought and analysis. Form replaced substance. PowerPoint became the method by which we think, rather than a tool to summarize and communicate our thinking to others. Critical decisions were made every day without the depth of analysis that the issues deserved. And in this shift, we began training ourselves to think in bullet points and sound bites.

Everyone got caught up in this. "We didn't take the step back and ask where the business logic was in this growth. Was it sustainable? That's where we lost our leadership, all of us, from CEOs to engineers," observes Malay Thaker, who has worked in Valley start-ups since 1987. In the atmosphere of hyperinflation, we convinced ourselves that the way business had been done for decades was no longer the norm, and that a new thing was happening. We stopped asking *what?* or *why?*—instead, we asked *when?* and *how much?*

The widespread fear that computer-controlled devices and network infrastructure would collapse on New Year's Eve 1999—the so-called Y2K problem—drove even more demand in the IT sector. No one, including the system developers themselves, really knew which parts of our infrastructure would be affected. All computer software that was written to store the date had to be tested and potentially rewritten.

The enormous size of this task, coupled with the time pressure, led to some of the early outsourcing of IT projects to India, launching the nascent tech industry there. The more advanced enterprises saw this as an opportunity to overhaul their computer systems and not just put in quick fixes to the date problem. But some vendors did not pay enough attention to the fact that the increase in purchases was being driven by a one-time event.

As we stood poised at the turn of the millennium, we were investing furiously in today's innovation, but not tomorrow's. What no one could anticipate was *how* important investments in the future would become to our national safety and economic growth.

CHAPTER 5

LOSING OUR BALANCE

The millennial fireworks displays around the world were amazing, and spirits were high. But the core values that had sustained our Innovation Ecosystem for decades had been gutted from within. Then three major shocks between 2000 and 2003—the bursting of the Internet bubble, the uncovering of a handful of corporate scandals, and the attacks on our nation on 9/11—threw the Ecosystem completely off balance. To make matters worse, these events happened at a time when attitudes toward science in the country were changing, making it even harder to recover.

In mid-2000, people began to realize that capital was neither free nor infinite; a business ultimately had to produce earnings. The disconnect between stock market growth and economic fundamentals inevitably led to a harsh reality check. The bubble burst, and Nasdaq fell. Internet start-ups that didn't have sustainable business models began to fold. Multiple Web sites were created just to gloat over the catastrophe.

When we started Packet Design in May of 2000, we did some great work with Internet service providers, analyzing their networks to identify key technical problems. Then, one by one, they started going bankrupt, and the people we were working with lost their jobs. The fall of the ISPs had a much bigger effect than the collapse of the dot-coms because of the magnitude of the amount of capital involved. The ISPs had been aggressively building out their infrastructure based on inflated demand numbers. The time came when the new service providers were not able to continue to raise funds without a clear plan for profits, and established companies like AT&T could no longer sustain the soaring growth rates.

As Nasdaq fell through the floor, investors large and small lost billions of dollars. To some this downturn was a return to reality, but to others it was devastating, as their life savings evaporated overnight. Recognizing the shift from a concentration of sophisticated investors to a base of shareholders who no longer worked through brokers, the SEC implemented new rules to ensure "fair disclosure." Regulation FD required that all public companies disclose material information to all investors at the same time. The SEC's intent was to bring more transparency to the investment process, but the result was that there was less useful data available for everyone, as companies became increasingly careful about what they were willing to reveal.

Everyone's risk profile changed. Large enterprises that had bought products from start-up companies now felt burned. Many of the companies that had sold these enterprises new technology could not provide support or went out of business. The service providers that had overprovisioned stopped buying completely, and the answer to any new proposal by enterprise CIOs was no.

Large tech companies like Cisco and Sun that had seen tremendous growth had to swiftly adjust to a new reality. Many of the small networking and software companies whose strategies were dependent on partnering with these larger companies had to adapt or fail. The Internet and technology industries that were the stars of the 1990s were suddenly not so popular among investors—or customers.

The venture capitalists, who had invested more than $54 billion in 1999 and $100 billion in 2000, had to take a step back, regroup, and figure out which companies could be saved and which had to be shut down. "They clearly went through a period of being risk averse, and that showed up in the limited amount of money they were going to put into anything," says investor Peter Currie. All their time went into their existing portfolios.

Biotech companies could no longer put together the $100 million plus syndicates of venture capital, pharmaceutical partners, and public market funds needed to fund basic research, development, and clinical trials. "Wall Street said, 'We're not going to fund basic science—we want to see products,'" recalls biotech investor Sam Colella. "Then Big Pharma said, 'We can't give you $50 million. We'll give you $5 million.'" Biotech VCs began looking for companies with short return horizons that could be financed relatively cheaply. In the early days of the biotech industry, probably 80 percent of Colella's most successful companies had been based on a major innovative breakthrough in science. But the type of science and research that he had previously funded was no longer financially viable. Investments shifted to start-ups dedicated to improving existing molecules and exploiting time-tested biological pathways using incrementally better chemistry or biology.

When the bubble burst, the pendulum swung to the other extreme. No one was willing to take risks, and without risk, there is no innovation.

TARRED WITH THE SAME BRUSH

As the stock market fell, the abhorrent behavior of a handful of companies came to light. When Jeffrey Skilling, the CEO of Enron (an energy company that had expanded into new markets during the 1990s), resigned in August 2001, many people wondered why, but few could imagine the magnitude of what was to come. A series of articles by a skeptical journalist and the resulting SEC investigation revealed grossly misleading accounting and multiple conflicts of interest within the company. This resulted in the largest bankruptcy filing in the country's history and a blizzard of indictments against Enron executives. As the company's stock price plummeted from $50 to pennies in less than six months, its employees lost not only their jobs, but also their life savings.

The feds also launched a fraud investigation against Arthur Andersen, the Big Five accounting firm that was supposed to provide the checks and balances on Enron. This investigation led to the dissolution of Arthur Andersen, putting more good people out of work. Then came the exposure of WorldCom's inflation of revenues and underreporting of costs in order to push up the price of its stock. WorldCom's bankruptcy in July 2002 was even larger than Enron's.

As these scandals came to light one after another, no one knew how deep the greed and malfeasance had gone, and everyone assumed the worst. Given the size of the companies involved—Enron, Arthur Andersen, WorldCom, Adelphi—the impact of these discoveries was huge. There was a pervasive loss of trust in all of corporate America because of the misbehavior of a few companies. Investors indicated this lack of trust by selling off their stock. The Dow Jones Industrial Average plummeted from over 11000 in January 2001 to less than 8000 in 2002.

There are some who clearly recognize the line between what is right and what is wrong and stand well behind it. Others go right up to the line. And then there are those who regularly and easily cross over, seemingly without guilt. The potential for great wealth combined with the pressure for continued stock market returns brought out the worst in those leaders who easily stepped over the line, along with some who were pulled across by standing too close. In the end, most people in the business world did no wrong—yet all were tarred with the same brush.

Firms that perpetrated fraud needed to face the consequences. But politicians, law enforcement agencies, and the securities commissions aggressively went after the executives involved in an overly sensationalized way that was designed to calm the markets quickly. Their actions were not always well thought through, and amplification by the media reinforced the growing lack of trust in corporations and their leaders. "There has always been a populist underpinning to American politics, and the dozen or so corporate scandals gave free rein to those bottled-up tendencies," reflects FedEx's Fred Smith. "It was like a huge echo chamber."

Less than a year after the first hint of corporate scandal, in July 2002, Congress passed the Sarbanes-Oxley Act (SOX). The 66-page legislation, passed with very few "no" votes, established new standards for U.S. public companies, boards of directors, management, and public accounting firms. For most companies, SOX did not change the substance of how they did business. But it added millions of dollars a year in expenses for compliance and legal fees that could have gone toward R&D and innovation. Innovations like building the next-generation data center could be justified only if they also boosted compliance. With CIOs occupied with making accommodations for all the new rules, enterprises stopped looking for big problems to solve.

The administrative and financial burden of SOX compliance was especially tough on small to medium-sized businesses. Companies found that they were doing more and more things for regulatory purposes, rather than because they made business practices more transparent. This made the path to liquidity for small companies even more arduous, making VCs even more timid about investing. It killed the dream of many entrepreneurs—that of taking their company public and maintaining their independence.

Shareholders became more active and vocal, demanding to know, "Where were the board members at Enron or World-Com?" With each new investigation, pressure was put on directors to show their muscle, eroding the critical trust relationship between shareholders and boards, and between boards and management. This new shareholder activism was not always informed by an understanding of the business implications of the things the shareholders were demanding. Suddenly, the nation was consumed by discussions of corporate governance processes—time that should have gone into discussions of business, products, services, and strategy.

There were also new regulations in investment banking that attempted to address real and potential conflicts of interest that arose during the bubble. A side effect of these new laws was that a lot of talent moved from investment banking into firms that were not subject to regulation, such as venture capital and hedge funds. "Some of the smartest people in business innovation are now working in hedge funds," says Google CEO Eric Schmidt.

The excesses of the dot-com era exposed weaknesses in judgment, controls, and regulations. But the overreaction of the country's leadership had the unintended consequence of creating an atmosphere in which boards and executives were less willing to take meaningful risks on products and business strategies. The real punishment was to long-term shareholder returns through a loss of focus on innovation.

THE AFTERMATH OF 9/11

In spite of the economic turmoil caused by the bust, our position in the world still felt secure. Then on September 11, 2001, we woke up to a nightmare, and with it we lost our trust in our safety as a nation. While the country had been focused internally, whether on the rising stock market or on political scandals, we were blind to the rising tide of hate for America around the world.

Within two months of the attacks, President Bush signed the Patriot Act. Many government-funded research projects were suddenly classified, limiting American scientists' ability to collaborate and share information with their peers around the globe. Some researchers even stopped taking funds from DARPA, becoming more reliant on the NSF. Scientists who were not U.S. citizens—even some who had lived in the United States for years—were prohibited from working with certain materials that could remotely be linked to instruments of terror. Visas for students and visiting scholars also became difficult to get, making it even harder to attract top talent.

We declared a war on terrorism to go after Osama bin Laden and al-Qaeda, and then sent our troops to Iraq. Just as a single-minded focus within a company has a negative impact on innovation, the war created a single-minded focus for the country, in terms of both the political debate and dollars appropriated. This focus limited the already scarce funds available for research and education and took political and public attention away from critical global problems, including climate change, sustainable energy, and health care.

The combination of less funding and a new leadership style at DARPA had a profound impact. The agency that had traditionally sponsored a combination of fundamental and applied research, depending heavily on the vision of its program managers, became more centralized.

As the capital markets opened up in 2003, enterprises began talking about innovation again and trying to figure out how to bring it back into their cultures. Many of the larger companies looked to acquisitions to enter new markets or bring in new ideas. But the support structure for start-ups had crumbled. The VCs began reinvesting, but their relationships with entrepreneurs were more adversarial. The core values of patience, risk, and trust had become scarce. The venture firms felt intense pressure from their limited partners to make up for the losses and excesses of the Internet bubble, which often resulted in counterproductive behavior. Suddenly, slips in schedule or markets that were slow to develop—common phenomena when dealing with high-risk start-ups—were no longer tolerated. Instead, these little speed bumps were used as an excuse to fire the CEO or recapitalize the company, often wiping out the early shareholders who took the initial risks. "We went through a nuclear winter that wiped out a lot of ideas, including things that probably should not have died," says entrepreneur Heidi Roizen. "Some of the companies founded during the bubble were dumb, but there were also smart companies in there that were just way ahead of their time."

For the first time in my career, I began to hear venture capitalists ask for customer references from companies that were not yet shipping product in order to "validate the market." My response each time was that by the time a market is validated, the larger companies are already competing for it, and it's too late for a start-up to succeed.

REVIVING INNOVATION

There is a disease that afflicts trees called root rot. Infected trees eventually die, but for a long time they appear to be healthy, with lots of branches and green leaves. Root rot is an apt metaphor for what happened to the Innovation Ecosystem as funding for scientific research declined. The time between the funding of research and the application of technology can be decades. We won't know—until it's too late—what branches and leaves may never grow because we neglected to maintain the roots. We've been neglecting the roots for some time, but since 2000, with the radical shift in the start-up environment, we have also been starving the branches.

The country's Innovation Ecosystem can still be revived if we act now. Businesses need to challenge the nearsighted focus being forced on them by Wall Street. We must expand our horizons, moving beyond incrementalism to encourage and value the deeper transformations required for future growth. We need the political system to work for and not against innovation, holding our political leaders accountable for making science a priority. The research foundation needs to be built up again, its structure reinvented in light of today's environment. To prepare our children for the twenty-first-century workplace, we need changes in education and culture.

Sustainable innovation will require sweeping changes at all levels of society—from the schoolroom and the playground, to the boardroom and executive suites, to the hallways of our nation's Capitol.

CHAPTER 6

GREEN-THUMB LEADERSHIP

The country's economic growth is driven by the health of companies large and small that are committed to researching, developing, and applying science and technology. These organizations must reexamine their Innovation Ecosystems if they are to compete in the global economy. Sustainable innovation will require extensive reform of leadership styles and company cultures, along with the support of the public and private investors.

For the last several decades, the intense focus on measurement and analysis has benefited those parts of companies that are process driven. Programs like Six Sigma are predictable and scalable, with sets of rules and structures that can be taught. Employees trained as Six Sigma "black belts" and "green belts" learn how to manage using acronyms like DMAIC—*define, measure, analyze, improve,* and *control.* But an obsession with optimizing efficiency while removing variations and defects is the opposite of what is required to encourage broad innovation.

New ideas and projects are delicate. If they are not given proper care and room to grow, even great ideas may not take hold. There is no one set of rules to facilitate leading for innovation. It requires intuition, imagination, and judgment, with decisions often needing to be made with little or no hard data. Leaders need to be supportive of experimentation and to have the natural curiosity and courage to try something new. But there are techniques that can be developed and lessons to be learned from the successes and failures of other organizations. Nurturing innovation is more like gardening than like karate. It doesn't require a black belt; it requires a green thumb. For organizations to thrive, they need a balance of both kinds of leadership.

ORGANIZING FOR INNOVATION

Large companies are process machines that are optimized to accomplish the core mission of the company. The bigger the company, the more rigid these processes tend to become, because by fine-tuning these processes, quarter-to-quarter results are maximized, generating short-term returns for shareholders. Management is, for the most part, about eliminating surprises. These organizations are like factory farms, dependably growing rows and rows of the same flower or vegetable, producing a set number of things at scale. Incremental innovation can be useful in this type of environment, but it is rare for significant innovation to occur under conditions of mass production.

To take root, innovation requires flexible, open, less hierarchical processes, with leaders who see their primary role as being supportive rather than directive. The most fertile organizations for innovation are typically very flat. Communication is unencumbered, and job descriptions are flexible. If you need to know something, you're able to go directly to the right person—literally or virtually—and ask. Not everyone is comfortable in this kind of environment, which tends to be more chaotic than traditional hierarchical organizations that are built to scale, and in which people know exactly what they're supposed to do.

CEO Eric Schmidt describes Google as poorly managed by design. Strong product managers lead dynamic teams of engineers, but "the teams are self-focused, and the level of control that we have over them is not great," he says. One day, he was surprised to discover that Google had a world-class group working on speech recognition. One of the managers had met them outside the company, thought they were really smart, and decided to hire them all without any idea as to what specific product they might build. Eventually, their concepts were incorporated into Google 411, a free telephone-based service that enables users to search businesses by phone. "If you had asked me if speech was important, I would have said that we should spend our money somewhere else," Schmidt admits, "but part of our culture is that the managers don't need to check with me."

Google's business model, combined with its market position and profit growth, makes this style of management feasible. Most companies can't adopt this approach wholesale, but the attributes of minimizing hierarchy while building a culture around flexibility and trust are key to innovation.

Organizing for both innovation and scale can be challenging. But it can be done if you identify those parts of the organization that need processes that scale, while aiming for an overall level of flexibility and capacity for change. To expand the horizons of our businesses, executives, boards of directors, and investors all need to understand that there is a time for applying disciplined rules and metrics and a time for trust and patience. Company leaders can't just treat innovation like a spice to be sprinkled here and there. Large companies have to make a commitment to having some pieces of the company that are outside of, yet still connected to, normal business processes. Like innovation greenhouses, there should be room in these units for playful experimentation and the right kind of nurturing environment to support disruptive change. Small companies need to resist the pressure to instill rigid processes as long as possible.

The soil of innovation is most fertile when the five core values are an integral part of the culture, people, and processes of the company. Employees need to be able to embrace change and recognize the necessity of looking beyond day-to-day execution. "I think the most important thing a CEO can do is to educate people that both operational focus and longer-term innovation are essential," says FedEx CEO Smith. "Remind people of what happened at Sears when it didn't pay attention to what Wal-Mart was doing, or of a moribund Apple being brought back on track by Steve Jobs. The ability to do that rests on the seeds you've sown before the organization needs a change of direction."

WORTH THE RISK

A willingness on the part of top management to be open about and tolerant of failure encourages people to take risks, to be up-front about problems, and to maximize learning from the experience.

Scale fast, fail fast has become the latest mantra among venture capitalists and entrepreneurs. It is a strategy that emerged from consumer Internet-based businesses that have the luxury of tinkering on the fly. The quest for instant success, however, can cause a company to give up on a slower-growing business that may need time to develop or adapt. A better approach for most businesses is to find ways to *fail early*, which may be the opposite of scaling fast. "We have built prototype vehicles from scratch in three months," says Danny Hillis of Applied Minds. "It is our smallness that lets us move quickly. We try out more ideas and are willing to make more mistakes."

Attacking the most challenging parts of a new project first may give you an early indication of whether or not the project is ultimately feasible. "If you can get past the two toughest chunks of it, then the others fall into place," says FedEx's Miley Ainsworth. "Find the ugly part—the part you don't think you know how to do—and that's the first part you attack."

In the late 1990s, Autodesk CEO Carol Bartz wanted to encourage the company to reduce its dependence on its original product, AutoCAD. She launched an initiative called Fail Fast-Forward. The central message to her employees was to try out new ideas and recognize failures as quickly as they could, but also to recognize the ways in which even a failure can move a company forward if everyone learns from it. At the time, AutoCAD accounted for nearly all of the company's revenue. Today, in part because of Bartz's initiative and subsequent cycles of innovation and acquisition, AutoCAD accounts for only about 40 percent of Autodesk's revenue stream.

The "scale fast" approach can even be dangerous in some sectors. The faster you ramp up the introduction of a product or service, the harder it can be to conduct the assessment and adaptation that is often necessary. The drug industry has become more aggressive in the introduction and marketing of new products, hoping that every next product will be a blockbuster. But this makes assessment through postmarketing data much more difficult, risking the possibility that unexpected adverse effects will be discovered only after millions of people are already using a drug. There is something to be said for a slower ramp, but it requires patience.

To create room for risk taking, you have to actively protect those who have been involved in a project that doesn't succeed beyond saying that they didn't get fired—this time. Too often, other employees want to punish innovators who fail, because they were competing for the same resources. "As a TV programmer, you knew that not everything you put on the air was going to work, and when it failed, it failed very publicly," says Disney's Bob Iger. "As business leaders, we have to measure people not only on if they have succeeded or failed, but on *how* they failed."

Genomic Health even threw a celebration for a project that was killed when a new technology didn't provide enough of an improvement to make it worth moving into production. "The project failed, but it was a great job by the team," says CEO Randy Scott. "We sent the message that it was okay, because we tried it. We need to know not only what works, but also the boundaries around what does not work."

Global auctioneer eBay has become an online powerhouse by tenaciously learning from its failures. The site experienced a number of technical glitches in its early days, and this eventually led the company to change its organizational structure, giving smaller teams more control over their own destinies. They developed a new back end for eBay.com that could handle more trading volume than the New York Stock Exchange and Nasdaq combined. Then, when the acquisition of PayPal put unforeseen demands on the system, they were able to address the problems quickly because "we had seen that movie before," says former CEO Meg Whitman. In a nondefensive atmosphere, failures can be analyzed with an open mind, yielding valuable lessons. "Mistakes are such a part of being better as a company," Whitman observes. "You learn a lot of from products that aren't as successful as you thought they would be."

A lesson learned from Apple's first foray into the wireless business was an important contributing factor to the iPod's unqualified success, according to former Apple senior VP Jon Rubinstein. Apple did not invent Wi-Fi, the protocol used to surf wirelessly at home, at work, and on the go. But the company made it available to mass-market consumers several years ahead of the PC industry. It integrated wireless cards into all iBook laptops, targeting students who wanted mobility. The company also marketed the sleek "base stations" called AirPorts that are required to connect wireless users to the Internet. Apple could have become a leader in the multibillion-dollar wireless access-point business, but at the time, it viewed the AirPort as just another way to boost Mac sales and declined to make the devices PC-compatible, shutting out the huge Windows market. "That was a mistake that I wasn't going to make again," says Rubinstein, who made sure that PC-compatible iPods were available within a year of the device's debut. "When we got to that decision point the second time, we decided that the iPod deserved to be more than a Mac-only product and should support both platforms."

Retrospective evaluations provide valuable lessons—*if* they're not just fancy PowerPoint slide shows highlighting the good and covering up the bad. "We conduct a formal postmortem independent of whether a given project was a failure or a success," says Anand Chandrasekher, senior vice president at Intel. "If you conduct postmortems only on failures, the process will get stigmatized and the organization won't end up responding well to them." By analyzing both successes and failures, organizations can learn to be more receptive and open to new initiatives, with no sugarcoating required.

Start-up companies and projects fail for lots of reasons. They can go out too early, or the technology may not be ready for market. The video-streaming technology of one of our companies, Precept, was ready—but the market wasn't. Now Internet video is everywhere. Cisco acquired the company in 1998 and has just begun shipping products that really leverage Precept's video technology. The barriers for customer trial or acceptance may be so high that even a great product can't get traction. Investors may get impatient and give up too early if the leadership of a company or a project isn't strong enough to sustain and communicate its vision.

It takes a special kind of resilience to get back up again after being knocked down. "If you don't, there are too many bumps in the road, and most people fall out before they ever get anywhere," says entrepreneur Heidi Roizen. If failure is a stigma, employees and leaders will not be willing to take the personal or professional risks required for innovation.

ENCOURAGING QUESTIONS AND OPENNESS

In companies large and small, questions should flow at every level starting from the top, from formal company meetings to hallway chitchat and online forums. Candid answers to these questions from executives set a tone for the whole organization. Framing the right questions when talking to customers, suppliers, and partners helps identify needs and root out potential problems. Innovation-friendly environments encourage challenging questions while discouraging combativeness and defensive attitudes that can shut down promising notions before they've had a chance to prove their worth. "You have to have a culture that is explicitly tolerant of the crazy idea, the criticism of it, and then its renewal," says Google's Eric Schmidt.

Open environments are not just about having open-door policies, but about encouraging people to share and be objective in self-assessment. New tools like instant messaging, wikis, blogs, social-networking software, and even virtual worlds can help organizations facilitate this sharing of crucial information, while enabling people in the organization to uncover internal resources that facilitate collaboration and synergy.

This openness also needs to extend outside of the organization. An overly inward focus can lead companies to make faulty assumptions in defining their products. When eBay developed a new service called eBay Express, which allowed customers to buy products more quickly without going through an online auction, it compared the service's performance to other areas of eBay itself, but not to other shopping sites. "I thought that eBay Express was going to be a huge home run, and it hasn't been," says Meg Whitman. "If you're going to have a more retail-like experience, it better be not just better than what's on eBay, but better than what's available off eBay. This experience has encouraged us to have a more outward-looking focus. If someone else has a better idea, we shouldn't stand on ceremony—instead, we should immediately adopt it as our own."

Encouraging employees to look at problems differently is a constant challenge, even at very innovative companies. A company's focus can limit its ability to see new opportunities. Today, if you talk about user-contributed content, few people think about Disney. But it was the first to come up with the concept in 1989, recognizing the trend of people using portable video cameras to record family events that were not only valuable keepsakes for posterity, but often hilarious. The result was *America's Funniest Home Videos*, which debuted nearly two decades ago. "Why is it that five years ago we didn't see that you could collect videos on the Web and create a site that mirrored the show, with a bit of a twist? But no one thought of it," admits Bob Iger. It took a start-up like YouTube to think orthogonally and apply the home-video concept to the Web.

The ability to think broadly is critical to innovation. "Too often people can't see beyond what their particular area is," says entrepreneur Jeff Hawkins. "People who are writing software don't think enough about how changing the hardware can solve a problem. Manufacturing engineers don't think about the implications of aesthetics and design." One way to broaden the outlook on a project is to encourage diversity of background and specialization on project teams. Microsoft's senior VP of research, Rick Rashid, stresses the value of "not only different expertise, but different perspectives as well." He makes an effort to include the points of view of anthropologists, psychologists, sociologists, medical doctors, physicists, chemists, and computer scientists from all over the world when tackling a difficult problem. Mixing things up can help people to gain perspective.

Start-ups are often counseled to focus their resources. But in my experience with early-stage technology and new markets, you first have to do some experimenting to know where to zero in. You need intense focus on the technical side to get the first version of the product ready, but then it's time to fan out and talk to customers in different market segments, identifying those problems that are ripe to be solved and the markets that are ready. Start-ups need to know when to focus and when to look more broadly.

Too much focus can also create missed opportunities for larger companies. These days, when investors have expectations of quick returns, many projects are killed too fast, before their potential value—or capacity to adapt—has been clearly ascertained. When companies are pushed to evaluate their businesses as stand-alone entities, it's important not to forget about the potential value of cross-pollination and synergy.

Being open to new ideas also means being willing to cannibalize your own product or business model before someone else does. The music industry could have benefited greatly by opening its eyes and changing its distribution models before Napster did it for it. The newspaper industry is currently ripe for such a quantum shift, says private equity investor Roger McNamee. "Fear of self-impact is what's killing newspapers. They're so focused on protecting their current model that they will not do the thing that their audience wants them to do, which is ultimately far more valuable than what they're doing now. The only way to fight the Innovator's Dilemma is to recognize that you're better off obsolescing your own stuff than having someone else do it to you."

In 1961, IBM made the bold move to make nearly every item in its catalog obsolete by designing a new operating system that would work for everyone. "It was a $2 billion, 10-year gamble that IBM won, and they dominated the computer industry for 25 years because of it," says entrepreneur Len Shustek, founder of the Computer History Museum.

FedEx is the company it is today because it has been able to continually revise and expand its view of its own core mission. After starting out as an overnight delivery company for business letters and light packages, it has matured into a company that provides time-sensitive delivery of items of all shapes and sizes by air and ground.

FEEDING THE BABY TIGERS

Companies—particularly successful ones—have a natural resistance to change and unintentionally create barriers to innovation. It is the job of the green-thumb leader to uncover and eliminate threats to new ideas and institutionalized barriers to their growth.

Promising projects that challenge business as usual are often either shut down up front or slowly bled to death by underallocating funds, management time, IT infrastructure, and marketing resources. "Senior management has to exercise its fiscal responsibility," says Bob Iger, "but that oversight can very easily stifle innovation, because the more systems you put in place to manage the spending of money, and the more bureaucracy you create, the more time it takes to get the work done."

Trying to fit innovative projects into traditional meeting and reporting formats can backfire by creating forums for the administrators to squash new ideas. Operations reviews focused on milestones and deliverables should be saved for later in the process, when monitoring a project's development or implementation. If you force operational metrics too early, few projects with the disruptive potential to create future growth will ever pass the tests.

Barriers to exploring new initiatives should be set low. Some companies establish so-called hurdle rates as a mechanism for vetting ideas and deciding what to fund. But financial metrics like hurdle rates and ROI (return on investment) need to be combined with good judgment and intuition. "If you're early in developing a truly new-to-the-world disruption and finance asks you for a spreadsheet predicting future revenue," Intuit's Scott Cook tells his employees, "do it in five minutes and then get back to figuring out how to solve the problem, because that's how we succeed."

New initiatives need to be actively protected. FedEx would not be able to offer its customers international express shipping or the ability to track and trace packages if the company's top management had not made a concerted effort to shield these projects from premature criticism when they were just getting off the ground. "If you don't protect your little scouting units, the regular army will devour them," says Fred Smith. Requiring that a proposed project or service have demonstrated demand can also kill off a company's future growth, he adds. "It's like saying there's not much demand for people crossing the Hudson River at 96th Street. You have to build the bridge there before there's a market."

Meg Whitman understands that a steady stream of new service offerings is crucial for eBay's future. She calls promising projects that are still gestating "baby tigers," and knows that they must get special care and feeding from management if they are ever to reach maturity. "We don't want the mother tiger to roll over and squish them, which can happen quite easily," she says. With a company the size of eBay, the already-established business can easily burn through an extra $5 million in marketing that may not actually create a measurable uptick. But $5 million can go a long way toward feeding a baby tiger.

One force that insidiously undermines the health of baby tigers is the tendency of small business units in large companies to feel that they are undervalued and of marginal importance. Any large and profitable venture tends to become obsessed with the business that led to its first success, which steals energy from the risk-taking, exploratory ventures that could turn into the next one.

Intel's decades of growth have come primarily from its dominance of the microprocessor market. Andy Grove famously proclaimed that microprocessors were Intel's "Job 1." The company's intense focus has led to excellence in the development and marketing of microprocessors, but it has not successfully entered new growth markets. "We look at the success of projects through the prism of the PC business, and that puts a lid on what is possible," acknowledges Intel's Anand Chandrasekher. Who would want to work on a project that's not considered top priority by management? But to achieve sustainable growth, companies must develop the capacity to nurture what could be *tomorrow's* Job 1.

Ignoring an opportunity because it is not a big business today is sure to stunt future growth. Questions like: *Is it a needle mover? Why are we wasting our money on this little thing?* are all too common in large organizations. These questions can stifle a new initiative that could end up being really big. "A lot of the companies that many of us started in the 1980s initially had fairly small niche markets, but eventually they became $200 to

$500 million market opportunities," says Audrey MacLean, a serial entrepreneur who now mentors the next generation of Silicon Valley leaders. Cisco Systems—with revenues of over $35 billion a year—started out as one of those niche players.

When the cholesterol-lowering medication Lipitor was first discovered, it was dismissed as not having enough market potential. Now it's one of the top-selling pharmaceuticals worldwide. Pedro Cuatrecasas led R&D in Big Pharma for several decades, and in a 2006 article called "Drug Discovery in Jeopardy" in *Science and Society*, he described successful products that nearly never made it out of the lab because of dour early sales predictions. During the development phase of acyclovir, a drug for genital herpes, the Burroughs-Wellcome marketing team declared "that there were 'no markets' for this compound." The $10 million estimate of peak sales turned out to be more than $90 million short for the drug eventually sold as Zovirax.

Fortunately Lipitor, Zovirax, Wellbutrin (an antidepressant), and Retrovir—which extends the lives of HIV patients—were all developed *in spite of* poor sales predictions. "The major lesson from the stories of the development of all of these drugs, which is repeated throughout the history of drug [discovery and development]," wrote Cuatrecasas, "is that nearly all drugs that have become blockbusters (and therapeutic breakthroughs— these normally go together) had similar early histories of major disinterest and skepticism from the commercial side, usually due to the misunderstanding of the marketing potential or medical need."

But not every new product needs to be the next blockbuster. "The genomics of the future is going to be about the science becoming more personalized for smaller markets," says former FDA commissioner David Kessler. "You don't do that in a blockbuster world." This will require adapting test methodology and developing new ways to identify the efficacy of a drug earlier in the testing process, such as measurement techniques that rely on molecular genetics to track the progress of specific diseases. In other areas, the Internet is being employed to uncover and precisely target smaller markets. Businesses from media to medicine need to look for new ways to match investments in development and marketing without compromising quality.

PLANNING FOR GROWTH

Developing a portfolio of innovation strategies for different planning horizons and building organizational structures to support the mix is like planning a garden that will be able to thrive in all kinds of weather. Biodiversity in a community of organisms is one of the surest signs of that community's health and ability to withstand shocks. The same is true of diversity of nascent projects in a company that is seeking to survive in changing economic conditions.

Each company should determine whether its crucial competitive advantages come from new technology, revised implementation, different distribution channels, disruptive business models, or some combination of these things. An innovation portfolio will be differentiated by the size, maturity, and market position of a company. It should reflect a variety of risk levels, balancing technical, organizational, and market challenges. Some companies can afford to invest directly in research. Every organization should ensure that it has the right partnerships with universities or start-ups to ensure an ongoing supply of disruptive ideas. You never know where innovation will come from. What is most important is that you have sufficient internal capabilities to build a network of relationships broad enough to touch the three communities of the Ecosystem.

Business leaders need to consider how to maximize innovation across three different time horizons simultaneously:

1. *Current generation.* Maintaining continual incremental improvement through product or process change as required to meet existing customer needs.

2. *Next generation.* Making advances in science and technology or business processes as required to maintain market leadership or to leapfrog competitors. These innovations might be incremental, orthogonal, or breakthrough.

3. *Future growth.* Even the most successful companies need to look beyond their current customers and markets to investigate potential areas of growth for the future. They also need to be prepared to take advantage of radical disruptions in their current markets.

The near-term horizons are driven by the needs of today's customers, and they should be the responsibility of every employee. FedEx has a corporatewide initiative that it calls the Purple Promise: each employee commits to making every FedEx experience outstanding. This shared mission encourages everyone at the company—from the employees sorting and delivering packages to those answering the phones, maintaining planes, and developing new IT systems—to make or suggest improvements every day.

The challenge when identifying areas of future growth is to free one's mind from the needs of today's customer and to think like someone who is starting a new business from scratch. "Mostly what we do is give people what they want before they know they want it," says Disney's Iger. "We need to be creatively innovative. If we had asked people 'Do you want to watch a pirate movie?' it is possible that 90 percent of them would have said 'God, no; that is yesterday.'"

The phrase *a technology looking for an application* is often framed in negative terms, but when you are looking for future growth opportunities, that may be exactly what you want.

Those working on future growth initiatives should be driven by what the company believes the market will be, not by specific customer requests.

Start-up companies have a clean slate from which to focus on future growth, and thus are the source of most significant product innovation. But once the first product ships, even young companies can stagnate if they don't continue to allocate resources to looking beyond the next product cycle.

How an organization supports these three horizons is dependent on its type of business, type of innovation, and level of maturity. Developers of semiconductors, pharmaceuticals or software, media companies, and health-care providers all have different operations cycles that influence how the fundamentals of innovation apply to their business.

Google's 70/20/10 rule explicitly communicates the company's portfolio strategy. Google invests 70 percent of its resources in the core businesses of search and advertising, 20 percent in new developments like Google News, and 10 percent in cultivating truly new ideas. The company actively encourages all of its engineers to allocate a portion of their time to unregimented learning or experimenting with new things—hoping that the next new great idea will emerge. "My experience is that most really strong technologists get excited learning about new things," says the company's senior vice president of engineering, Bill Coughran. "It's healthy for their professional development and for the health of the organization."

Combining current- and next-generation product development in this fashion works best for companies that can add a feature to a product, get feedback, and adapt at relatively low cost. But even for those companies that have long, capital-intensive product cycles or that have to face complex regulatory hurdles, leaving time in employees' schedules for them to explore new ideas, build productive relationships with their colleagues, or attend conferences can boost the innovative potential of the business as a whole.

One of the most effective ways to focus on the future is to create small, dedicated teams or strategy groups, granting them the freedom to develop their own rules, structure, and culture, but enabling them to leverage the resources of the company as a whole. These groups can be long-term organizations or temporary and mission-driven, disbanding when they have served their purpose. To create the iPod, Jon Rubinstein launched a virtual start-up within Apple. He staffed this task force with both engineers chosen from inside the company and fresh talent brought in from outside. "This gave me the opportunity to build an improved methodology with a hand-picked team from the very beginning that could have a slightly different way of approaching the problem," Rubinstein explains. "I didn't want to distract the mainstream teams from getting Macs out the door."

Another motivation for establishing separate forward-looking groups is that they require a different leadership style. "The way you manage a very large product group like Windows or Office doesn't apply very well to a riskier activity," says Microsoft's Rick Rashid. "The kinds of choices you train managers to make are not the choices you want people to make in areas where you're expecting them to take a lot of risks, and where the value of what they're doing isn't so much for the current revenue as for the opportunities they're trying to create for the future." Typically, managers are trained to be risk-averse and schedule-focused, which is not appropriate for projects that aim to stretch the company's mission and goals. "Product development and research are two different things, and mixing them diminishes them both," says Intuitive Surgical's Gary Guthart. "If you mix research into product development, your products are always late or always over budget, and there's an enormous amount of uncertainty, because you're basically saying, 'Please invent on a schedule.' Everyone knows you can't invent on a schedule."

In 1997, Peter Hart—one of the few Westerners to serve as the executive officer of a major Japanese corporation—launched a group called Ricoh Innovations to bring a Silicon Valley perspective to its parent company, an established maker of digital cameras, copiers, fax machines, and other imaging products. RI does a mix of applied research, advanced development, and investing, aiming to create new technologies and cultivate business opportunities that will drive Ricoh's growth. Essential to this mission are flexibility and freedom from fixed schedules and daunting bureaucratic procedures.

"Corporations need a place where smart people have no schedule of deliverables and can abandon something if they get a better idea," Hart observes. "We have no formal procedure. No one has ever had to write a proposal. Anybody can propose a new project or project area at any time. First, we're in brainstorming mode, when all you have to do is build the idea. Then we get critical and evaluate the idea along several dimensions, like risk-reward ratios and how much technology headroom there is. If we do it, will anybody care? If something looks like it's in the sweet spot, and resource requirements are reasonable, we say, 'Yeah, go do it.'"

In recent years, many companies have created "innovation officers" and special teams to emphasize their commitment to the future. If set up right, these groups can be effective in championing new efforts and facilitating companywide collaboration. But they can backfire if they act as gatekeepers, introducing new barriers instead of removing old ones. A commitment to innovation starts with the CEO and is every employee's responsibility.

ACQUIRING INNOVATION

Strategic acquisition has become one of the most potent techniques for growing a business. By incorporating smaller companies that have come up with disruptive ideas and already tested the marketplace, large companies can gain an edge on the future.

Larger corporations will benefit from cultivating the right reputation with smaller companies, which often assume that they are just being milked for new ideas. To a little start-up, a large company is the 800-pound gorilla. Even initial discussions could tip off potential competitors to what they're doing. People whose job is not to exploit, buy, or replicate, but instead to listen and become the champions of new ideas, are more likely to convince smaller companies to share information, leading to mutually beneficial relationships.

For Cisco, mergers and acquisitions are a central aspect of the corporate strategy for growth. As of July 2007, Cisco had acquired 121 companies. I experienced this process from both sides. One of my own start-ups, Precept Software, became the company's twenty-third acquisition. Then when I became Cisco's CTO, its mergers and acquisitions teams reported to me. Key to the company's success was learning how to evaluate and integrate acquisitions.

Like Cisco, eBay has also concluded that much of the company's truly evolutionary innovation is probably going to be acquired from outside. "It's unlikely that we're going to come up with the next Skype inside of eBay," says Meg Whitman. She cites the company's acquisition of PayPal as another successful example of this strategy. "There's something magical about a small number of entrepreneurs, motivated by the potential of a buyout or a long-term IPO, who are truly disruptive thinkers," she says.

Companies that become too dependent on external innovation, however, can find themselves without enough internal talent even to make the right decisions as to what to acquire. Great scientists and engineers want to be surrounded by their peers. Without a commitment to some level of internal innovation, it's hard to recruit and retain the best talent.

SHORTCHANGING THE FUTURE

The intensified competition and reduced margins of the current business environment threaten investments in future growth. "Most of us have gotten trapped by our own business models," says Autodesk's Carol Bartz. "We're expected to make a lot of money so we can take our 90 percent gross margins. But it's a shame we couldn't take 10 of those points and do more research, because we've allowed ourselves to be bound by expectations and become victims of our own success."

When things are going well, it's often hard to imagine that they won't continue to do so. In today's world of compressed time frames, some companies choose to ignore the future-growth horizon, believing that in a climate of rapid change, it's impossible to predict what will be. But this is even more reason to devote resources to anticipating future scenarios and technologies, so that you'll be prepared when you need to react. "As an established organization, you have to be able to look at both *now* and *then*, or eventually you will come under extreme pressure due to technological change or the emergence of a new competitor that's got a different process or approach to the market," says FedEx's Fred Smith.

In the mid-1980s, Intel made a bold move that ended up saving the company—exiting from the declining memory business and focusing on microprocessors. But that move was possible only because a small team at Intel was already developing microprocessors. "Because of an accident that we had nurtured, we had an option," says Andy Grove. "We used the catastrophic condition surrounding our first business to force change."

Investing in the future now is like buying insurance, giving you the potential to adapt. Dedicated resources might take the form of an internal advanced technology group, a strategy team that is constantly scouting for new technologies and acquisitions, or research scientists collaborating with universities.

Most corporations cannot undertake the broad research agendas of the past. But more focused applied research can and should be done, either internally or through partnerships with universities, in strategically selected areas that could make or break a company's future. "People running companies need to be pretty merciless in what areas of research they choose," says venture capitalist Mike Sheridan, "but they also need to really figure out what they have to excel at in order to survive." Internal research organizations can translate directly into long-term shareholder value by exploring areas that may prove crucial to the company in the years to come. Researchers can also provide valuable insight and expertise that can enable the company to fix problems and enhance products more quickly, thus gaining a competitive edge.

The corporate research organizations of today can no longer afford to run like the ivory-tower labs of the past, centralized and isolated from the mainstream business. Instead, they should be porous, providing tight connectivity with the rest of the company.

When Hossein Eslambolchi became the CTO of AT&T in 2001, he tried to change the mindset of AT&T's scientists, asking them to think of themselves as one-third physicists as they wrestled with theoretical issues, one-third engineers, and one-third businesspeople, so that they would think more deeply about the customer experience. "You want to think about the future, but we had to get the labs more engaged in dealing with customers and give them the ability to analyze real production data," he says.

Leading research requires a very different skill set from running other parts of a company, including significantly more patience and trust. When Robert Spinrad became the second head of Xerox PARC in the late 1970s, he knew better than to tightly manage the group. "I would hear about things that I thought were really way out, but I bit my tongue," Spinrad recalls. "I assumed that half of the stuff we were doing wouldn't pan out. But I never knew *which* half."

For all its dominance of the PC world, Microsoft has not traditionally been considered an innovative or open company. But today, Microsoft is one of the few IT companies that has both the market position and the long-term outlook to support a large-scale research lab. "The very first part of our mission statement says that our goal is to further the state of knowledge in the areas that we do research. There is no reference in that goal to Microsoft," says Rick Rashid, who has led the lab since 1991. Its funding comes from the corporation itself, and it doesn't cost anything for a product group to leverage the lab's expertise, so there is no disincentive to working with it. Microsoft's executives see the lab as a crucial source of the company's capacity for change.

"One of the reasons a company like Microsoft would want to do research, as opposed to just advanced development, is that it gives the corporation an agility that it would not otherwise have over the long haul," observes Rashid. "It allows us to change rapidly under conditions of stress, because if we face a new competitor or a new business model, or a new technology arises, chances are good that Microsoft Research has already been working in that area for ten years."

Some leaders today have an aversion to the concept of separate groups committed to basic research, seeing them as an antiquated organizational structure. "The research stuff on the hill is death," says Eric Schmidt of Google. "It may be a good model for someone else—though I doubt it—but it's clearly a bad model for us." While the technologists at Google Research do selectively publish papers, their more advanced work is not released to the larger scientific community. Google Research is tightly integrated with the core business, which keeps it tethered to real-world needs. But without open collaboration with universities, the work performed there doesn't benefit the Ecosystem at large. Those companies that don't have an internal research organization benefit from active engagement with the larger research community—an interaction that is critical to maintaining the health of the nation's Innovation Ecosystem.

IDEAS EVERYWHERE

Viable seeds for growth can be found at all levels of an organization, from the senior executive level, to newly arrived interns, to the client-facing sales force. Leaders should actively foster channels of communication that encourage people to bring ideas forward, and establish mechanisms for capturing, vetting, and prioritizing those ideas. These channels can take the form of face-to-face conversations, casual brainstorming sessions, or online tools, where employees are encouraged to make suggestions without fear of reprisal or premature evaluation. Organization charts often insert too many layers between people with good ideas and those with the power to authorize their exploration.

In start-ups, it is typically the leaders who set the direction for the company. Each of the companies I launched with Bill Carrico was inspired by academic research that led us to imagine how the technology could be used in a new type of product. At Bridge Communications, we leveraged the Ethernet and protocol work done at Xerox PARC and Stanford. Network Computing Devices built a graphics system around the X Windowing System developed at MIT. Precept's video-streaming software was based on collaboration between Lawrence Berkeley Labs and the Information Sciences Institute at USC. But as companies grow and diversify, it is the rare leader who can continue to generate all of the new ideas. In fact, if too many ideas come from the top, employees can quickly learn that they should stop trying to innovate, because the boss's ideas are going to trump anybody else's.

At Google, thoughts about new features and products are discussed broadly via e-mail on an "ideas" list and at informal brainstorming meetings. Experts are brought in daily to give talks at the company on a wide range of topics to provoke employees to think about problems in new ways. The day I visited the Googleplex, an astrophysics expert was discussing the likelihood of finding life on other planets. "All of these are just mechanisms to make people comfortable with throwing new ideas into the pot," says senior VP Bill Coughran.

There is no substitute for leaders spending time talking and listening to their employees. Demonstrating that new ideas are being considered and discussed is the best way to encourage people to speak up. Not every idea is good, and not all good ideas can be implemented. But when people don't feel that they're being listened to, they shut up.

The process of choosing *which* new ideas to fund needs to be clearly articulated and transparent, whether the final decision is the responsibility of the product teams or of top management. Buy-in is important, but requiring consensus slows things down and doesn't always result in the wisest decision. There is always someone who is willing to play devil's advocate and say no. It is easier to get consensus on projects that are more predictable and less truly innovative.

At Applied Minds, the first test of a new idea is a gut-level one: is the proposed project something that people would feel good about working on? The second test is economic, a classic risk-reward analysis. The third test is whether or not the employees believe they would do a better job of executing the project than anyone else. These three tests are applicable to all types of businesses. Providing modest levels of seed funding for employees who are passionate about an idea is a good way to ensure that worthy projects don't fall through the cracks before reaching the point where they can be evaluated.

"We always want to have more great ideas than we can work on," says Nathan Estruth, general manager of Future-Works, a division of Procter & Gamble (P&G). Having a multitude of new ideas in the queue enables the company to pause if a particular idea proves to be too challenging for current development. "We may end up putting an idea on the shelf with a note that says, 'Here's one we couldn't solve,' but maybe someday we'll come back to it. We have that luxury because we know there are other ideas, just as exciting, waiting behind it," he says. Having more good ideas than you can work on leaves room for serendipity. You never know when a change in strategy will make one of these temporarily "parked" ideas invaluable—or when such an idea might inspire you to rethink your strategy.

Just as in a real garden, it's important for a green-thumb leader to identify the projects to prune and thin—which require instinct, judgment, and a bit of luck. By necessity, organizations that have trouble weeding out unpromising projects put up high barriers to launching new initiatives. The flexibility of the people that you hire, the ways in which you choose what to fund, how you set expectations, and how you terminate unsuccessful projects all affect how readily an organization will accept the pruning and thinning that are essential for maximum growth.

Employees—particularly in middle management—can become overly protective of their pet projects, even when it's clear to everyone else that it's time to call it quits. They may be afraid that they will lose their position in the organization altogether, or be viewed as a personal failure. People should be rewarded for stepping up and acknowledging that it's time for their project to be cut back.

At HP Labs, a pattern emerged when the company looked back at the research projects that had been transferred successfully to product groups. The average time that the successful products had taken to go from the lab to the marketplace was five years. The managers agreed to a funding commitment of five years for new projects. If a project had been going on that long and had not yet been transferred, either the manager had to explain how much more time was needed or the researchers would be expected to work on something else. "It became a very useful tool," says Joel Birnbaum, who was director of research. "People had in their mind that if you didn't do it in five years, you were going to have to explain why. Your project wouldn't necessarily have to die, but you were on probation, and there either had to be something very special about what you were doing, or you were kidding yourself."

Outside of the research community, leaders can't always afford to leave it up to the team to decide when to move on or whether to wait. Making sure that you have accurate information about a project—its real status and the obstacles it faces— is critical to making the right call. Often, this can be gleaned only in informal discussions with the teams. How you make the decisions to prune or thin, and the method and tone of communicating the necessary course correction, will have impacts on new ideas throughout the company.

CREATING INNOVATION MAGNETS

Household and health-care products giant Procter & Gamble (P&G) has a strong commitment to innovation. Its research labs around the globe employ more Ph.D. scientists than all the Ivy League universities combined. A division of the company called FutureWorks—funded by an "innovation board" made up of P&G's top executives—coordinates internal development efforts and forms strategic partnerships with outside companies and independent inventors. FutureWorks is an idea shop, a product incubator, and a vehicle for harnessing the innovative energy of start-ups. "We recognize that disruptive innovation is advantageous as part of our overall growth portfolio," says Nathan Estruth, general manager of the division.

Employing experts in R&D, manufacturing, sales, finance, and market research, the aim of FutureWorks is to create new platforms that can mature into billion-dollar businesses in three to ten years. "By working across all these functions, we're able to look at new business ideas on what we call the three legs of the stool—the consumer, the technology, and the business model," says Estruth. "We identify the challenges and killer issues and work against those."

P&G has a companywide partnership initiative called Connect & Develop (C&D). When the company faces a business or technical challenge, it consults with its C&D experts to find a solution, leveraging collaborations with research groups, business units, and universities. Monthly conference calls keep FutureWorks up to date with developments all over the world. "We're constantly discussing what's hot or new, and highlighting technological discoveries that could have broad application across our business," Estruth explains. "Some of the magic around our innovations is our ability to be at the nexus of that information."

FutureWorks' portfolio includes projects with a heavy R&D emphasis and others that are focused on changing business models. A joint venture with a company called Inverness Diagnostics to provide rapid at-home diagnostic tests is now an integral part of P&G's health-care unit. One of the projects that is still incubating is a partnership with MDVIP, a health-care company based in Florida that focuses on personalized wellness and disease prevention.

One of the ambitious projects that didn't work out for Future-Works illustrates the importance of identifying potential barriers to success up front. P&G was excited about partnering with a company called Songbird that makes inexpensive, disposable digital hearing aids. Dramatically changing the lives of those with mild to moderate hearing loss represented a huge market opportunity for the company. "People who started using Songbird couldn't imagine life without it again," says Estruth. But the company ended up being stymied by the FDA and faced a five- to ten-year, multimillion-dollar process to gain approval. "We still are owners in the company and remain passionate about the idea, but it was one of those projects where we anticipated the wrong killer issues," Estruth admits.

Attracting innovation from outside gives P&G a decisive competitive advantage. Estruth conceives of FutureWorks as an "innovation magnet" providing mutual benefits for P&G and its many partners: "If they can maximize their value, we're going to win, and the consumer is going to win as well." By setting up a separate internal organization to leverage external creativity, Procter & Gamble has created the best of two worlds, combining the global resources of a multinational corporation with the idea engine of the start-up world.

THOSE WITH CRITICAL OPTIMISM

"Innovation is massively dependent on the skills of the individual," says PayPal cofounder Elon Musk. Each stage of the process requires people with a particular set of talents and skills. At the core are those who have the passion, curiosity, and inclination to experiment. "You can put your shingle out and say that you've now got an 'innovation team,' but if you put the wrong kind of people in there, you will not be successful," observes FedEx CIO Rob Carter. "But those who are able to innovate successfully seem to be able to do it time and time again."

Innovators need to be what I call *critically optimistic*—enthusiastic about their projects, but also open to spotting potential problems and making necessary course corrections. "It is the ability to critically assess and optimistically improve that makes for better professionals, better companies, and better countries," says Joost CEO Mike Volpi.

The ability to identify needs, to frame questions, and to feel comfortable with ambiguity are all required in the early stages of innovation. "One of the things I've noticed about myself," observes Applied Minds's Danny Hillis, "is that I really enjoy working on something when the problem isn't defined yet, and getting to the phase of 'We got it working!' Then my enthusiasm starts trailing off. But there are a whole bunch of other people whose interest ramps up at that point."

Those are the people who can help you follow through on a great idea. Heidi Roizen started a company called T/Maker in 1983 to develop application software for the nascent personal computer market. T/Maker introduced a simple clip-art application called Click Art that ended up being the dominant brand in that space. "At every trade show, someone would come up to me and say, 'I had that idea too!'" Roizen recalls. "So many people had the same idea, but we did it—and in just nine weeks, from the day we thought of it to the day we had a product on the shelves."

Today's products are so complex that the stereotype of an innovator inventing the future in his garage no longer applies. "Twenty years ago, someone could create a product all by themselves," says Jon Rubinstein, "but today that is just impossible. So teamwork is essential, not only between people, but between companies." Teams should be small, dynamic, and flexible, while still being in touch with the company's overall mission and community. A well-matched team of five to eight people can outperform a group of a hundred. Best Buy has adopted the strategy of creating small, temporary networks to tackle specific projects, drawing people from diverse areas of the company. "A lot of our networks have been created by individuals," says VP Kal Patel. "We encourage them."

Many companies are starting to recognize the power of these informal networks in boosting creativity. In truth, *every* company has an informal organization inside it that is how things really get done. Leaders should nurture the proliferation of these unofficial lines of communication, while being careful not to formalize them to the point where they become as cumbersome as the formal structures they are working around.

Relationships in an Innovation Ecosystem require a deeper level of interaction than the traditional transactions in the business sphere. Collaboration is not just about meeting deliverables, but about defining opportunities for mutual benefit in terms that all parties understand. People who naturally play the role of *knowledge connectors* are critical when building relationships across communities, disciplines, or divisions, facilitating communication between disparate groups. The best connectors can quickly synthesize information across a broad range of topics, communicate well, and bring the right people together, while having no overriding agenda of their own.

The technology transfer team at Microsoft Research was created to keep track of what the developers and researchers are doing and foster collaboration between groups. "It's a lot like generalized matchmaking," laughs Rick Rashid. "It's like they're running a dating service—they help find mates and, when necessary, even do couples counseling."

Because their successes are often happening in the background of specific projects, connectors need to be identified and protected. "These people often have the most institutional knowledge across the company," says Ellen Levy, managing director of Silicon Valley Connect. "They do a little bit of everything, but because they don't have specific deliverables, you think you wouldn't necessarily miss them tomorrow if they were gone. That's wrong."

Opportunities for acquisitions or partnerships that could bring benefit to multiple businesses within a company often fall through the cracks because no one is willing to champion or pay for something that will be shared across the company. Levy calls this the "integrator's dilemma." Connectors can help resolve this problem by bringing issues to the attention of management, increasing buy-in across the various groups, or making everyone aware of the potential benefits of the deal.

Sustainable innovation requires fostering working environments where people are at liberty to think and act like entrepreneurs—even in big companies. The most successful entrepreneurs question norms, learn to operate with low budgets, stay flexible and agile, quickly integrate external feedback, and focus on the goals of the project at hand more than on company politics or organizational status. Executives and managers need to inspire and encourage that spirit in every employee, no matter how large their companies are.

INCENTIVES FOR SUCCESS

Leaders can communicate their vision and values all day long, but if the incentive systems in an organization are not aligned, innovation won't happen. Typical compensation structures targeted at driving short-term results need to be reexamined in light of their impact on collaboration and risk taking.

"If you overimpose metrics, you sacrifice creativity and open thinking," says Joost CEO Mike Volpi. "You have to be thoughtful about how hard you drive those metrics, because they can be innovation killers." Metrics-driven bonuses are easy to implement and understand, and are effective when focusing on yearly financials and incremental improvements. But they need to be complemented with programs that reward behaviors that are not measured in a spreadsheet, recognizing and rewarding value creation in addition to today's revenue and profit.

It's hard to create precise incentives for *potential* value. But employees need to understand the benefits of investing in the future, even if it affects this year's earnings. "You have to convince people that if we *don't* do these things, we're not going to have long-term opportunities," says FedEx's Fred Smith. "It's more an issue of leadership and communications than it is of measurement and quantitative systems." Companies that combine annual bonuses with stock-based incentives can increase their employees' personal investment in the growth of the company.

Management must always strive to be fair and equitable in its pay structures, but "fair and equitable" should not be confused with "uniform." Attracting and retaining top talent might require paying some people more than others for doing a similar job. Or it might mean providing a level of flexibility to accommodate individual styles, outside interests, or family life. "In schools, we give kids anything from an A to an F, which is a pretty broad range," says Volpi. "In corporations, you basically get either a B or a C."

As organizations grow larger, it becomes harder to leave room for recognizing and rewarding special talent. This is one of the challenges now facing union leaders and corporate management—enabling employers to provide fair compensation for all, while allowing leeway to encourage innovation through extra incentives if necessary. It is worth being creative if you want to hire and retain the best.

Raises, bonuses, and promotions should encourage teamwork while still reinforcing individual accountability. Leaders need to recognize how their systems encourage or discourage risk taking—in part by differentiating different types of success. "I'll take a person whose project succeeded technically but didn't get any traction in the business," says Ricoh's Peter Hart, "and I will give them a bonus and say, 'That was a fantastic accomplishment.'"

Rewarding employees for taking the time to push forward ideas that do not have a direct impact on their jobs, or giving them credit for launching projects even if they weren't involved all the way through, doesn't always have to come through the standard compensation structure. Having a way for employees to spontaneously recognize their peers for less tangible achievements can raise the team spirit of the company as a whole. At FedEx, managers use a program called Bravo Zulu—named after the maritime tradition of flying B and Z flags to signal admiration for sailors in another vessel—to reward and inspire extra effort, with cash awards ranging from fifty to several thousand dollars. It's a simple but effective system to reward those who may not automatically get credit another way.

Incentives come in many forms, both formal and informal. How you pay, promote, and praise employees are all explicit ways of reinforcing performance. Employees also carefully gauge the behaviors of those who get listened to most often and funded more easily. In cultivating innovation, implicit signals from leaders are as important as explicit ones.

OPEN AND OUT

Companies are relying more and more on outsourcing and partnering to compete more effectively. Organizational and geographical borders are yielding to a global, mobile workforce. Engineers and scientists are forming mutually beneficial networks of expertise that transcend institutional boundaries.

One of the most effective demonstrations of the power of distributed intelligence is the open-source software movement. By enabling programmers all over the globe to directly participate in software development, open sourcing has created a class of worthy low- or no-cost software products like the Linux operating system and the Firefox Web browser. But while open sourcing can enhance incremental innovation by drawing on talent outside the corporate mainstream, relying solely on the wisdom of the crowd rarely leads to the next great disruptive idea.

Leveraging talent in other countries via offshoring can cut costs and speed the development process. It also invites a diversity of cultural perspectives and brings new ideas into play. But distributed intelligence needs to be applied cautiously to the process of innovation. For products that are well defined, the assignment of labor to far-flung groups can be relatively straightforward. Forcing this discipline too early can limit the kind of broad-based exploration that thrives in face-to-face interactions and in fruitful collaborations among engineering, marketing, and management. For companies with advanced technology groups, it's best to create networks of complete teams, as opposed to just offshoring a piece of the development. Companies that farm out all of their entry-level jobs or the production tasks that were traditionally allotted to junior employees may eventually discover that they have offshored their next generation of leaders.

WHEN, HOW, AND WHERE TO TRANSPLANT

A key factor in gaining economic benefit from innovation is how successful we are at transplanting ideas, inventions, prototypes, and products within and between the various communities of the Ecosystem. Even the healthiest plants can die if they are not transplanted with care.

The style of transplanting needs to be adapted to the type and stage of innovation. Transferring technology from academia to industry is very different from bringing new products to market. Integrating acquisitions and scaling internal development projects each have their own challenges. Products that are consistent with existing businesses and customers are easier to scale than those that will push the company into new markets.

Intel's inability to evolve beyond the microprocessor business has not been due to a shortage of great ideas at the company or an inability to scale. Instead, Intel has a *transplanting* problem—an inability to migrate projects from the lab bench to the marketplace. Andy Grove acknowledges this. "We had the world's second digital camera, we had all of those spin-offs, but we did not suck those ideas up and cultivate them," he says. "Whatever it takes, we're lousy at it."

Xerox was able to successfully transplant printing technology from its labs because it fit an existing business model. But its historic failure to capitalize on the astonishing innovations in computing developed at PARC was a different story. As part of an early strategy to get into the general-purpose computing business, Xerox bought a company called Scientific Data Systems for hundreds of millions of dollars. The acquisition was a spectacular failure, and the company decided that it had made a blunder by trying to enter the computing business.

When PARC researcher John Shoch tried to sell management on turning the lab's technology into marketable products, he wrote a prescient memo describing why the company should be selling high-performance, single-user, programmable workstations—an early version of what we would now call a PC. "I got a call from some meatball at corporate staff," Shoch recalls. "He told me, 'John, I figured it out. You want to be in the computer business again.' Xerox had the second largest office-equipment sales force in the country, but it didn't have a *computer* sales force. This conditioned the thinking about what products the company was willing to sell. The systemic failure was that all of that great research and thinking had been done in the context of a copier company, rather than in the context of a computer company."

Determining precisely when to transplant a project is crucial to its success. Isolating a project for too long can create walls that limit its ultimate acceptance by the rest of the organization. But trying to scale too soon can cut off the ability to adapt quickly to feedback.

Whenever you take a small company and make it part of a larger organization, the natural instinct of the larger organization is to try to reinforce the processes that have made it successful. In absorbing the new organization, the parent company often immediately tries to change the ways in which the acquired company gets things done. You have to look closely at how each company does development, manufacturing, sales, and support—and then make wise decisions about which should be integrated into the parent company and which should remain the task of the smaller organization. If the new project does not share technology or markets with current parts of the organization, it may be best to let it grow independently.

"When I was at Cisco, we tried to recognize which of the larger corporation's business processes should be instituted as the dominant one, and the ways in which the smaller company needed to be protected," says Mike Volpi. "On a case-by-case basis, we would do an analysis and say, 'For this company, I think sales, customer support, manufacturing, human resources, and IT can be blended together, but we should keep product management, marketing, and engineering separate.'" Simply assuming that everything should immediately make the transition to the large company's way of doing business can end up killing off what you acquire.

When Google acquires a start-up, its smaller teams are often quickly integrated into the engineering culture at large. But a modest acquisition like the satellite-imaging firm Keyhole—which developed a major chunk of what became Google Earth—was allowed to run on its own for a while. "They were in our building, which gave the company a chance to try and figure out which pieces of Google were interesting to them as they began to integrate with our other products and systems," says senior VP Bill Coughran. YouTube was allowed to retain even more of its own identity, he adds. "The site has explosive growth that we don't want to disrupt in any way. So it's really up to the YouTube founders to decide when they want to integrate."

Often transplanting only ideas or technology alone doesn't work—you have to be able to transfer something more ineffable but equally important: "If you don't have that central passion, you don't have anything," says Autodesk's Carol Bartz. "That's why what we like to do is to make *people* acquisitions—to grab their thought processes. We have managed to buy some great technologists through small acquisitions."

I learned this the hard way. We launched three start-up companies from the advanced technology work we did at Packet Design, LLC, and the most successful company was the one that inherited the majority of the original team. Sometimes you will not be able to transfer some of the initial team members, because they will not always fit in well with the new organization. People who are great at leading early-stage projects and companies are not always good at transplanting and scaling. Many advanced technologists and researchers are not going to be happy working in a company that is focused purely on development.

In these cases, it's better to map out a temporary arrangement that enables people to aid in the transition phase, then go back and work on something new. At Sun Microsystems, people work in the labs for a few years to get their project to the stage at which it can be prototyped. Then they migrate to one of the business units, where their project can be produced and delivered. "You see it out to market and then come back to the labs and start again," says chairman Scott McNealy.

Successful transplanting of innovation takes various forms. It's crucial to know when it's the right time for a product to leave the lab to be produced in volume and sold. It's equally important to know when it's time to acquire a new company that is carrying seeds of innovation in it, or, if you're a smaller company, to know when it's the right moment to *be acquired*, so that your good ideas can take advantage of an established production and marketing infrastructure that will spread them widely in the world. Key to the success of a particular innovation is knowing when and how to integrate it into the organizational mainstream. But most important of all is having committed leadership.

REBUILDING THE ENTREPRENEURIAL ECOSYSTEM

The growth of the U.S. economy has become dependent on the small, innovative companies that have thrived for decades in places like Silicon Valley. These start-ups depend on passionate entrepreneurs, forward-looking venture capitalists, and open-minded customers, all of whom are willing to take risks and try new things.

One of the effects of the Internet bubble, however, was to raise investors' expectations about exit strategies. "Ultimately, the venture model is capped by the magnitude of the exits, and if you get only one billion-dollar exit every three years in the whole community, it's not going to work," says Heidi Roizen. "You have to have multibillion-dollar IPOs to make this business work, and our market is not currently healthy enough to support those."

Because of SOX regulation, companies now have to be larger to go public, so more companies are opting for getting acquired instead. This means less job creation and limits the VC returns, creating even more tension in the start-up environment. "People don't understand how delicate and complex the entrepreneurial ecosystem is," says Roizen. "They don't understand that some of the things you change don't show their impact for many years."

As money poured into VC coffers in the 1990s, firms had to take on many more partners. A lot of these new recruits were really bankers who thought they understood technology. "It's not so much that these people were not smart, it's that they were not traditional venture capitalists," says entrepreneur Joe Kennedy. The old-style VCs thought of themselves as good judges of character who could spot and nurture potential in people and companies. These less sophisticated investors tend to replace experience and instinct with a rule book. Believing that there is a recipe for success, they try to impose fixed processes on small companies, which is exactly the wrong approach for early-stage investments. "Now venture capitalists really see themselves as money managers," says Steve Goldby, executive chairman of Symyx Technologies. "They compete to get into a company, but just as they get in, they're focused on getting out."

Thus, known quantities and already established business models are favored over the truly innovative. There is too much money in the system now going after the same markets, trying to figure out where the next Google or Facebook will come from. With groupthink the order of the day, the VC landscape has taken on the appearance of a peewee soccer game, with everyone running toward the same part of the field.

Even more experienced VCs are taking fewer risks. Now you have to not only have identified a need but be able to assure investors ahead of time that customers will buy your product. "People are looking for much more customer feedback faster today," says longtime VC Wes Raffel. Start-ups used to *create* markets, not just serve them, and the VCs were happy to invest in anticipation of a new market taking off. The current hyper-cautious approach may be good for the venture capitalists' short-term returns, but it is not good for their long-term health—or for sustainable innovation.

In the past, not every venture had to be a home run. In today's environment, if the ball isn't immediately slammed out of the park, investors lose patience. "The gestation period on the deals has changed," notes entrepreneur Audrey MacLean. "Nobody expected you to have $70 million of revenue in less than five years. But now $70 million is considered puny. And five years— who has that long to wait? It's a very impatient model."

Ideas that require longer development periods, or that seem to be out of the mainstream, are less likely to get funded. "The people who want to be hard-core technologists are being shunned by venture capitalists," observes VC Yogen Dalal. "They say, 'We don't want to be agents of change. We just want great returns.'" Fewer start-ups are capable of producing true paradigm shifts, and those that aim that high are struggling for funding.

The crucial conviction that "the only way you can be a failure in Silicon Valley is not to have tried" is now at risk. "Having been a participant in a company that failed is a much bigger stigma than it was in the past," says VC David Liddle. "There's a lot more blame game now." Instead of recognizing that the occasional failure is the price of having high ambitions, investors see more luster in having played a minor role in a spectacular company than in having tried to build something significant. Learning how to manage difficulty is what start-ups are all about. If it was easy, anyone could do it.

Individual investors— "angels"—are a great source of funding for very early ideas. But the venture community needs to embrace the concept. Today's term sheets often contain provisions that wipe out the angels who do not have the capital to participate in future rounds. Those who are willing to take risks and provide seed money should not be discouraged.

Unfortunately, the entrepreneurial ranks have also changed. The passion and tenacity that built Silicon Valley have been replaced by entitlement and impatience. In the Valley's early days, engineers leveraged their own inventions to launch new companies. Not anymore. "When hype and marketing took precedence over substance in the investment community, that really changed the tone of things," says entrepreneur Martin Eberhard. "You wound up with business model innovation instead of product innovation. But in the end, you have to have something to sell."

The ability to launch and steer small companies toward big successes is in danger of becoming a lost art. For years, I have been hearing VCs say that their greatest challenge is finding the right leaders. "The real commodities are the CEOs," says VC Bob Metcalfe. Where are the young leaders who want to invest their hearts and souls in building something that changes the world—not just their net worth? Many entrepreneurs who would have dreamed of going public in previous eras no longer have that option. And others no longer want the pressure or liability of running a public company, opting instead for instant liquidity through acquisition.

On a more positive note, some of the seasoned VCs who want to give back to society and recognize future opportunities are now funding ventures in the areas of sustainable energy and the environment. But in many cases they could end up financing primary research. "The flood of funding into the green world is encouraging, because in order to make substantial progress, we will need fundamental breakthroughs," says entrepreneur Len Shustek. "My concern is that I'm not sure they're in for the long term. Are they willing to invest in a project that might take ten years?" he asks.

To make a difference, some of these technologies will require infrastructural changes that only very large companies or the government can provide. "Right now we're seeing energy deals that are really quite early-stage from a returns perspective, but are getting just unbelievable valuations. It has the potential to blow up," says Forest Baskett, general partner at New Enterprise Associates. This is such an important area for our future that we need to invest wisely to avoid creating a "green bubble" followed by an inevitable backlash. VCs should pick companies in the development and application communities, such as those offering solar solutions or energy-efficient products, that are more aligned with their investment time frames. The federal government should be called upon to pull its own weight on the research end, and not assume that industry can do it all.

Overall, I am not confident that we learned the right lessons from the crash and burn of the previous decade. Trendiness in deal valuation still reigns supreme in the Valley. Both entrepreneurs and VCs need to stop and remember what happened the last time that substance was sacrificed for hype.

Venture capitalists should look in the mirror and ask themselves if their investments are consistent with the high-risk, high-return, company-building strategies expected of their funds. They need to relearn how to nurture the companies in their portfolio without getting in the way of management. Their limited partners also need to have patience and recognize that we cannot compensate for the losses of the bust without seriously compromising the future. And entrepreneurs need to understand that starting a company is risky and hard work, not an easy road to riches. Founders should be passionate about building companies that have value for the long term, while being open to serendipity if the right suitor comes their way.

IN THE BEST INTEREST
OF THE SHAREHOLDERS

A CEO serves at the pleasure of the board of directors, and both are responsible to the shareholders. The interests of all groups should be aligned to create long-term growth. But investors' desire for faster returns, diminished trust in the boardroom, and shorter CEO tenures have combined to make it hard to define what the "best interest of the shareholders" means.

Knowing how a company is using its capital is key to making informed decisions. But each quarter must be put in perspective. "We have an economic system that is all about quarter to quarter, and the result is incrementalism that is driving away innovation," says Bill Carrico. "Why are General Motors and Ford failing? They can't get the really jazzy new things out because they're trying to build the incrementally better Ford pickup instead of hybrids like Toyota."

Businesses are judged on their earnings per share (EPS) or their return on investment (ROI), both of which are measures of today's results. In today's fast-paced, unpredictable business environment, perhaps a new measure of value should be added to our roster when evaluating a company or organization— its CFC, or capacity for change.

More people own stock than ever before, but they own it for a briefer time. The 24/7 business media have turned the race for short-term gains into the financial equivalent of a sport. Temporary downticks and lengthy development times are not tolerated. Placing value on investments in R&D is becoming a quaint relic of a more hopeful past. "There was a time when GE said 'Progress is our most important product.' Its stock would go up if it spent more on research, because the coupling between R&D and business value was so obvious back then," says VC David Liddle. "But people don't believe that anymore. Everyone is a flipper. People don't hold stock; they buy stuff in the morning and sell it after lunch."

In a world of exponentially accelerating change, Wall Street is demanding yearly returns that are accurate to the penny. "That's the reason we've stopped innovating," says scientist John Seely Brown. "We have indeterminacy being watched by ultradeterminacy."

Private-equity buyouts of public companies release those companies from the pressure of meeting the Street's quarterly expectations. But the companies end up under mountains of debt, and suddenly every staff meeting is focused on how to pay the interest on the loan. Without very committed leadership, taking a company private can be counter to innovation, forcing management to obsess about short-term financials instead of exploring new products and strategies.

Boards of directors don't serve the shareholders by trying to be managers. But openness, curiosity, and appetite for risk in the boardroom can be a decisive factor in a company's freedom to innovate. There's a Delaware law called the Business Judgment Rule that is intended to allow boards to make the best decisions for their stockholders without constant fear of litigation. The drafters of this law understood that courage and boldness in the face of risk are at the heart of good business.

Under intense scrutiny by shareholders and the press, fear of loss of reputation creates tension in the boardroom. When trust runs thin, questioning turns judgmental, management becomes defensive, and innovation is edged out. "The focus is to keep your company out of trouble and to check the squares," says retired Lockheed Martin CEO Norm Augustine. "I've sat in board meetings where we had major decisions to make, listening for hours to experts telling us what could go wrong. You couldn't help but think to yourself, 'If I vote against this, there's no downside. But if I vote for it and it goes badly, we could all end up sued.' The motivation for boards and management is to vote against things that may entail risk, even if the risk is clearly on the record."

In a world of revolving-door executives, swapping out the CEO seems to be many boards' knee-jerk response to a declining or slow-growing stock price. Senior managers can no longer assume that they'll be at the helm for long, which encourages even more shortsighted thinking. Why should they make bold decisions for the long-term health of the company if they'll be history in three years—the current average length of CEO tenure? And why should boards stand firm alongside their CEOs to invest in projects that might not show a profit for years, under pressure from "flipper" stockholders demanding instant returns? Why? Because our future depends on it. Our society as a whole is growing risk-averse. But by trying to predict and prevent every failure, we end up quashing innovation.

Today we point and click to order food, buy a book, watch a video, or pay our bills. But the Web would not exist had it not been for federal grants to universities and corporate research labs, risk-taking VCs and entrepreneurs, and companies and individuals who welcomed this new way of sharing ideas and doing business. People take magic like this for granted. "In the environment that exists today in the United States, we're designing more and more barriers to innovation, every day, right before our eyes," warns Bob Iger. The barriers are being created inside of organizations, in the national infrastructure, and in the culture in general. We must bring our national Ecosystem back into balance.

CHAPTER 7

REVIVING THE NATIONAL ECOSYSTEM

Innovation is not important just to the business community. The quality of life that we're accustomed to, financially and socially, is dependent on growth. If one person's gain is seen as another's loss, optimism, openness, and generosity are replaced with self-protection and fear. But economic growth alone will not provide us with a bright future. We face significant challenges—in energy, the environment, health care, and security—that pose serious threats to our way of living, while also providing significant opportunities for innovation.

As a country, we are spending and creating value elsewhere, rather than investing in our own growth. In 2006 alone, large drug companies doubled their R&D investments in China and India to $2.2 billion. Our culture has become focused on short-term financial transactions at the expense of building for the future. In 2000, the United States led the world in the adoption of broadband Internet, but seven years later, we ranked sixteenth. Large corporations now buy innovation from small start-up firms. But these new ventures depend on a level of risk taking that is no longer there.

The number of foreign students studying physical sciences and engineering in U.S. graduate schools surpassed the number of American-born students in 2000. Universities in other countries conduct engineering and business classes in English to attract faculty and students, while America puts up barriers to entry. The future does not look bright, as the United States ranks seventeenth among nations in kids that finish high school, and fourteenth in the percentage of students that earn college degrees.

Science and innovation are inextricably linked, and those who are able to learn, understand, and apply scientific knowledge will have an increasing advantage. The late astronomer Carl Sagan said, "We live in a society exquisitely dependent on science and technology, in which hardly anyone knows anything about science and technology." Overall, the country is not adequately prepared to deal with the complexity of the issues that are facing us. Saturated with problems, we expect other people—particularly politicians—to solve them. "Technology has become so overwhelming, at such a bewildering pace, that people feel threatened by it, and react by viewing science as being either beneath them or too hard and geeky," says Eric Haseltine, former chief scientist for the Director of National Intelligence and now president of Haseltine Partners. As a nation, we have become antiscience at a time when we need science the most.

The government of China has a 15-year plan for tying 60 percent of the country's overall economic growth to scientific and technological innovation. Our country's investment in innovation comes out of discretionary spending, which is being dramatically reduced as more and more dollars go to supporting the war in Iraq. It's sad to think that the current generation of Americans may, for the first time, leave behind a legacy of a lower standard of living than they themselves enjoyed. "Should that occur, it will be the consequence of a collective failure to respond to the increasingly clear signals that are emerging, and indicate that we have entered a new era," says former Lockheed Martin CEO Norm Augustine.

Opportunities for innovation are all around us, in every field of science, education, and health care, and in the application of ubiquitous connectivity to all aspects of our lives. "This is the best time," says SRI's Curtis Carlson. "These are not hundred-million-dollar opportunities, but multi*billion*-dollar opportunities." He has christened this nexus of increased opportunity, intensified competition, and an accelerated rate of technological change *the exponential economy*. We need to be able to move fast, but the increased pressure should not reduce our patience for things that take time.

Meanwhile, other countries are aggressively positioning themselves for the future. "China is where we were in the early 1960s, and they look at us as the big Sputnik target. They are very hungry, and not so concerned about immediate economic payback," says Eric Haseltine. To maintain economic growth, we need to reinforce our unique strengths, focusing on where we can excel and add the most value. We will never be the low-cost provider, but we can lead in innovation. Our strength is in our ability to work across all the communities of the Innovation Ecosystem—discovering, developing, and applying new ideas, products, services, and business models. No other country can offer the kind of infrastructural support for innovation that we can, from venture capital, to bankruptcy laws that make it possible to restart after failure, to our higher education system.

But the most important resource we offer is our freedom. "We outinnovate much of the rest of the world largely because we are free to do so," says Intuit's Scott Cook. "People can reach their own creative potential and not be constrained." As we look to set policy or improve education, we must recognize these unique strengths and not rush to merely imitate what other countries are doing. Educational systems that work in a more structured society may stifle the creativity and cognitive liberty that produced decades of innovation here at home.

Reviving America's Innovation Ecosystem will require us to think beyond the next quarter or election cycle. We need to increase our focus on acquiring new knowledge and information from the research community. We need to regain our appetite for risk in the development community, enabling us to take that new knowledge and translate it into useful products and services. And we need people in the application community—individuals, medical professionals, and educators as well as government and corporate employees—who understand enough about science and technology to be able to apply it. This is possible only by realigning the environmental factors that support innovation. It will take change in the nation's leadership, an assessment of a broad range of policy, and a major reinvestment in research. We need a strong commitment to raising the science and technology literacy of all of our children.

We all need to think like innovators—to identify our real needs, frame the right questions, try things, assess, and adapt. Like all innovators, we must not allow ourselves to be daunted by failure. The core values of innovation—questioning, risk taking, openness, patience, and trust—should be our guide.

WE ARE NOT ALONE

Accomplishing this mission will require a different type of approach from what we are used to. America has dominated the rest of the world in innovation for decades, but we are no longer alone. "If you add up the population of India, China, Korea, and the former Soviet Union, Russia and all the Baltic states, that's about 2.5 billion people," says former AT&T CTO Hossein Eslambolchi. "If you assume that 10 percent of those people are educated, that's 250 million people—twice the size of the U.S. workforce from an innovation perspective." Historically, America has set the agenda, expecting everyone else to follow, and we are not used to sharing the spotlight. Those days are over.

Just as the success of every organization is dependent on a thriving national Ecosystem, the United States is part of a global Ecosystem of innovation. Great new ideas travel around the world at the speed of light. Simply because a discovery occurs in America does not mean that we will be the sole beneficiary of that discovery. As other nations grow in power, a U.S. ban on a particular area of research will not prevent it from going forward; it will simply guarantee that the research occurs elsewhere.

A zero-sum view—assuming that progress in the rest of the world is a loss for us—creates a *fait accompli*, leading to more barriers and stifled possibilities. In the end, we all lose. The answer is to open up, creating networks of talent that cross international borders. Unlike military power, economic strength is not a contest or a race. "Growth in the rest of the world is a good thing for us as well," says leading economist Paul Romer. We can no longer afford to think in terms of us versus them, which results in a focus on short-term competition rather than long-term progress. The end goal is growth and making the future better than the past, so we must think of us *and* them, enabling the benefits of innovation to flow worldwide.

As an entrepreneur, I learned early on that you don't need to be the biggest in order to lead, but you do need to be smarter and more agile, and to know how to leverage the resources around you. We must be prepared to compete with other countries for talent and investment while understanding that they are also our allies. We have to learn how to collaborate and play well with others. This will take a more inclusive and interactive leadership style than we've had in recent years, and it requires us to feel stronger and more secure. It often seems easier to be a bully than to be a facilitator.

We need to be open to collaboration not only in science, but also in setting policy. Businesses, nonprofit organizations, state legislatures, political parties, and countries must communicate and listen to one another. Many of the significant problems we face are increasingly complex and global in nature. In learning how to work together again as a country, we can take lessons from industry.

FedEx offers express, ground, and freight delivery services, each with its own organizational requirements, but the company does not let that hinder its ability to use the combined strengths of its businesses to compete as a single company. FedEx's strategy of "compete collectively, operate independently, and manage collaboratively" could be applied to the United States as a whole. In such key areas as education, the states will need to collaborate, so that we can innovate and compete collectively as one nation.

We need to learn to give and take, share information, and leverage the expertise of others. "If we don't start asking ourselves, 'How do I build bridges?' or 'How do I build a framework in which dialogue is possible?'" says Google's Vint Cerf, "we're going to find that people with completely different world models will be unable to understand each other and that tensions won't resolve well, which could turn into some very serious problems."

While in Washington to testify on behalf of a cap-and-trade system, one CEO was asked privately by a member of Congress if he thought that a U.S. decision to follow the Kyoto Protocol limiting carbon emissions would hurt his profits. The CEO's response was, "Sir, my company works in 58 countries, and in 56 of them, we have to obey the Kyoto Protocol." The growth of American corporations increasingly depends on the rest of the world, and they're beginning to figure out how to be better global citizens in ways that also bring economic benefit.

A VACUUM OF LEADERSHIP

A healthy Innovation Ecosystem requires leadership that provides vision and an environment of openness and trust. Instead, the country is being led by fear, religious ideology, and partisan politics. Even those entering public service with the best of intentions have a hard time making a difference.

Our national imperative has become the War on Terror, a single-minded focus that has resulted in invasion of privacy, an immigration clampdown, and billions of dollars spent on war. When fear becomes the driving force in a society, people stop asking questions instead of looking to the world around them for insight and collaborative potential. When you shut off questioning, you constrain thinking. The prolific innovation in the 1970s and 1980s came from people who were educated in the 1960s—a time when people actively questioned authority.

We must break this cycle and mobilize the nation by encouraging empowerment rather than helplessness. There is a tendency to overreact in the interest of national security, but we must be very careful about deciding when to classify or withhold information. The power of information is magnified when it is shared, creating a network effect. Innovation is proportional to the level of collaboration and sharing.

The Bill of Rights begins by defining the separation of church and state: "Congress shall make no law respecting an establishment of religion or prohibiting the free exercise thereof." But fundamentalist forces that have too much influence on the nation's leadership are threatening our first freedom. While religion does not have to be at odds with science, religious doctrine often is. Einstein declared that "the cosmic religious experience is the strongest and the noblest driving force behind scientific research." He rejected the doctrines of theistic religions at the same time that he said that science without religion is lame and religion without science is blind.

Decisions to fund or restrict scientific inquiry or school curricula should not be swayed by religious ideology. Critical areas of science like stem-cell research are used as partisan footballs, instead of being developed to the point where they could save thousands of lives a year. Science does not belong to the right or the left, but the hijacking of science policy as a political tool has had a chilling effect throughout the Ecosystem. "We are a religious society, and to many people of faith, science gets used as a club, so their interest in supporting a lot of basic science is low," says Netflix's Reed Hastings.

Our first freedom provides room for the diversity of beliefs that are the fabric of our nation. "Separation of church and state helps us create an open society with the best the world has to offer," says Intuit founder Scott Cook.

The country has become more and more polarized. It's hard to expect others in the world to trust us when we don't seem to be able to collaborate within our own borders. "Washington is the most partisan I've seen it," says Norm Augustine, who was assistant secretary of the Army for R&D in the early 1970s. "I've been in and out of the city since 1965, and there is a growing attitude that politics is a zero-sum game. There is rancor, bitterness, and lack of cordiality beyond what I've seen, and that's tragic." Many politicians are aware of the issues we face, such as the need to upgrade our educational system, solve the problems of energy dependence, improve health care, and reignite innovation. For years, the partisan debate over the existence of global warming has taken precedence over efforts to begin addressing the problem itself. These are tough, long-term problems that do not attract short-term voter support. "The local political issue trumps the national interest," says FedEx CEO Fred Smith. "That's a very bad environment in which to innovate."

Legislation that will affect future generations should not be based on the latest polls. Just as customers often don't know what they will need in the future, people can't always see beyond their current needs and desires to identify what is right for the country or the planet in the long term. Many people not only are unprepared to think about science and technology, but don't understand their relevance to daily life. That's why we need leaders who seek advice from experts and take the time to understand and think through the impact of their decisions. This may seem unachievable in today's polarized environment, but Congress, like a national board of directors, needs to remember that its primary responsibility is to the country's long-term prospects.

The role of a nation's leaders is to foster the right environment for innovation through inspiration, funding, and policy. Our national deficit is out of control, but too much federal funding is spent inefficiently, devoted to areas of lesser importance— or to war. With real assessment and courage, we can find the funds to invest in our future. The necessary cultural changes cannot be mandated or imposed by heavy-handed bureaucracy; they must be nurtured and allowed to grow. Leadership can provide the spark, but change of this magnitude requires marshaling the country's people and businesses. "We need people to buy into a vision of how science and technology can offer them a better life," says Richard Zare, professor of chemistry at Stanford.

We must reduce our dependence on oil for both economic and strategic reasons, and find alternative energy sources that are clean, scalable, and affordable. With our global partners, we need to maintain the health of our planet's ecosystem, turning the tide on climate change and protecting scarce resources, while not compromising technological and economic progress. Rising costs and changing demographics of age and wealth distribution require new models for making high-quality, affordable health care broadly available without limiting advances in medicine. We must protect our country from those who wish us harm, while working to treat not just the symptom, but the disease itself—a growing hatred for America and what we stand for. And we must do this without giving up the freedoms that are so central to who we are.

Each of these four challenges should be a wake-up call equivalent to the launch of Sputnik by the Soviet Union in 1957, and each deserves a heroic effort—its own "moon shot." Rallying the nation's entrepreneurial spirit around these will enable us to tap the best minds in science and technology. Each moon shot will require ongoing discoveries in research, new products from the development community, and behavioral change in the application community. We will need both incremental improvements and long-term disruptive solutions.

IS ANYONE IN D.C. LISTENING?

All areas of federal policy need to be reevaluated in light of their effects on innovation. Research funding, K-12 education, tax incentives, immigration, and the policies of the FDA and the patent and trademark office—even the research and management philosophies of the DARPA director—all make a difference. Decisions about scientific, environmental, and health policies should be based on the best data available, rather than on data that happen to support the current administration's policies. "It's scary to think that decisions of great moment, of national and global import, are being made without adequate consideration of fundamental science and technology," says Vint Cerf.

Currently, eight of China's nine top leaders are engineers, and the ninth is a geologist. Contrast this with our own legislature:

less than 5 percent of the members of Congress list their occupation as being in medicine, science, or engineering, while 40 percent are in law. We can't expect all of our elected officials to be scientists or engineers, but we can demand that they respect and value good science as the foundation of sound national policy. We should expect them to use state-of-the-art knowledge as they make their decisions as the guardians of our future. Science should not be traded off against the political considerations of the election cycle. "We need to bring back into government a system that knows science can help people and that uses it to help inform policy decisions," says Susan Wood, former director of the FDA's Office of Women's Health, "rather than a system that thinks of scientists as a political pressure group that can be listened to or not, depending on the day."

Several organizations exist to provide scientific input to Congress and the executive branch; they were created to support budgeting decisions and help understand the implications of legislation. The president has a science advisor who runs the Office of Science and Technology and oversees committees of outside experts, including the President's Council of Advisors on Science and Technology (PCAST). But the advisor needs to have a real seat at the table and not be there just for show. PCAST should be staffed with people who have diverse scientific expertise, experience, and perspectives, independent of political agendas. "In recent years, the president's science advisor has been moved more and more out of the cabinet-level role, and has become a technician—a person whom you go to for an answer," says Robert Spinrad. Why shouldn't the science advisor have a role in discussing the affairs of the nation, as does the secretary of state or the secretary of the treasury?

Special committees are the primary mechanism by which government agencies get input from the scientific community. Under the Federal Advisory Committee Act, these groups are supposed to represent a balance of views, and should not be inappropriately influenced by any special interests. For the past eight years, in areas ranging from environmental policy to reproductive health, these rules seem to have been forgotten. Selective interpretation of data to support political positions is not new, but Susan Wood observes that "there is pretty widespread agreement that there has been a fundamental shift in the nature of how this has happened. This is different in both scale and kind, happens much more often, and is much more blatant."

When Richard Carmona resigned as surgeon general in 2006, he testified before Congress that his work had been consistently interfered with by the executive branch and its appointees, saying, "Anything that doesn't fit into the political appointees' ideological, theological, or political agenda is ignored, marginalized, or simply buried. . . . The problem with this approach is that in public health, as in a democracy, there is nothing worse than ignoring science or marginalizing the voice of science for reasons driven by changing political winds."

The consequences for government agencies, from NASA and FEMA to the EPA and the FDA, have been devastating. These agencies exist so that the rest of society can go about its business with confidence that there will be safe and effective drugs on the market and federal assistance in times of crisis. When the foundations of our society start to crack because scientific and technological competency have been shunted aside to cater to a particular political constituency, we can no longer trust the areas of government that assure our quality of life.

A FRESH APPROACH

These problems are sufficiently severe that incremental change is no longer enough. Given the background and focus of our political leaders and the increasing importance and complexity of science policy, we need a fresh look. One approach would be to remove core science policy, such as funding allocations, key staffing recommendations, or even health-care policy, from the political process altogether.

The complex decision making required for setting short-term interest rates is delegated to an independent institution called the Federal Reserve System. The White House and Congress are not involved in monetary policy, because their time is consumed by responding to short-term political pressures, which leaves them little opportunity to think about the future. "We created this elitist institution and delegated decision making in this very critical area to it," says economist Paul Romer. "The Fed looks quite broadly and systematically at these issues in a way that doesn't happen on science and technology policy." We should consider setting up an organization, analogous to the Fed, with the mandate of advancing science and technology policy in the interest of sustainable innovation. We could base such an agency on one that already exists—the National Academies.

Abraham Lincoln launched the National Academy of Sciences in 1863 to "investigate, examine, experiment, and report upon any subject of science or art" on behalf of the government. The NAS and the National Academy of Engineering, Institute of Medicine, and National Resource Council are collectively referred to as the National Academies. This institution serves the government as a prestigious panel of independent experts with nonpartisan objectivity. It leverages expertise throughout the country, relying on scientists who volunteer to serve on their own time.

The members of the National Academies are careful not to cross the line from science into advocacy. They have a level of credibility that is hard to maintain in Washington. But this strength is also a loss for the nation, because we are not taking full advantage of the resources that this esteemed organization could provide. The National Academies is primarily reactive to the executive branch, Congress, or agencies that are willing to fund studies. "It has independence in the sense that it is a private institution, and can choose a topic to comment on and say unpopular things," says MIT's Dave Clark. "On the other hand, the organization doesn't have a line-item allocation from the federal government, so it doesn't study something unless somebody pays it."

With changes to its charter and funding mechanisms, the National Academies' National Resource Council could play an expanded role in setting policy and allocating funds. This would require the NRC to have a membership sufficiently diverse in expertise and age to meet this higher level of responsibility, and a mechanism to include input from all of the three communities of the Ecosystem into the scientific discussions. We would also have to make a long-term commitment to a level of funding available to the NRC that it could allocate to such areas as research or education. By providing real independence, long-term leadership, and sustainable funding, we could remove short-term political pressures from critical decisions influencing our future.

While we work toward long-term disruptive solutions for the problems we face, we also need immediate incremental change. At a minimum, the National Academies should be provided with more discretionary funding by government or greater industry and philanthropic support, so that the organization can be more aggressive in restoring science to the top of the national agenda. Being more proactive would enable it to identify areas of concern and be ready to generate advice on a timely basis. Instead of waiting for marching orders from the executive branch or other agencies, the institution could be investigating topics that its members think are important—or are soon likely to be. "We need to be playing more of an early-warning radar role," says Charles Vest, president of the National Academy of Engineering. "We shouldn't have to wait until someone asks us to do a study." By then, the problem under examination may have already gotten out of hand.

"Our system works better than any other country that I know of," says Robert Spinrad, "but it isn't good enough to solve the problem of getting the government to understand that science should be supported as part of the cultural basis of a society. It can't be fixed by tinkering. It needs a major reset at the top level." Our leaders and legislators must open their ears and minds and solicit input from experts, learning how government can accelerate innovation while enabling innovation to change government. Key positions—such as the director of the National Science Foundation, the head of DARPA, and the secretary of energy—need to be filled by people who value science, technology, and the long-term view, independent of partisan agendas. Most importantly, policy decisions must take into account whether they encourage or discourage the core values of innovation.

PEOPLE POLICY

The communities of the Ecosystem need to be able to draw on a diverse pool of scientific minds—people with math or science degrees who go into teaching, business, or law, along with practicing scientists and engineers of all types. Everyone should have the same opportunities, but people are not all the same. There are some who are brilliant, some who have more aptitude and interest in science or technology, and some who are more creative than others. We need to be able to attract and retain the best.

Diversity is one of our country's great advantages. Since its inception, America has benefited from a massive transfer of intellectual property into the country through immigration. Of the venture-backed public companies started in the past 15 years, one in four was created by people who came to America from somewhere else. Today, these companies employ an estimated 220,000 people in the United States. "We're a country of immigrants," says professor Richard Zare. "It was easy for us to panic after 9/11 and decide that letting foreign elements into the country was tantamount to admitting potential terrorists, but to our detriment, we've greatly overdone this."

We want to attract the very best and brightest to come here to study, and then go on to interesting careers in academia or industry. "It's so scary to leave your country, leave your language, leave everyone you know, and immigrate. You're not going to do that if you're lazy," says Intuit's Scott Cook. "You are only going to do that if you're really a go-getter, and in most cases, we benefit like crazy." Whether people stay to build new lives here or not, increasing global engagement in science and technology via immigration has been a positive factor for our economy and our standing in the world. Each student who comes here from a different nation and culture brings greater understanding, and with greater understanding, perhaps more hope of peace.

As our requirements at home grow, there are not enough Americans to meet the demand. We are building barriers to entry just as opportunities in other countries are increasing. "The need to immigrate to America is waning," says Sequoia Capital's Michael Moritz. "If you're young, ambitious, and adventurous, and you grew up in Delhi, the impetus to come to America is diminishing, because the opportunity increasingly will be on your back doorstep."

It's hard for us to attract students when they don't have confidence that they will be able to get visas to work here. Immigration policies have put arbitrary caps on the number of knowledge workers we let stay each year. The number of H-1B visas is so restricted that in 2006, the limit of 65,000 visas was reached even before the year began. "We can't get smart people into the country anymore, so we have to have them essentially as refugees outside the country," says Google CEO Eric Schmidt. Additional uncertainty has been created by the Defense Department's emphasis on funding projects for which international students are ineligible because they're not U.S. citizens. Denying temporary visas for visiting scholars in the name of security has limited collaboration and the flow of ideas, and has forced important scientific meetings to be held outside of the country. "The United States has become much less hospitable to the intellectual classes all over the world," says Princeton astrophysicist Jeremiah Ostriker.

A few years ago, at a FedEx board meeting in Shanghai, I sat next to a customer at dinner who had been born in China, went to school in the United States, and stayed to work for 10 years. He had come to Silicon Valley because that was where the excitement was, but now he's back in China because he believes that's where the excitement is. "We used to import talent; now we export jobs," says Hossein Eslambolchi. The more we export jobs, the less attractive it is for future innovators to come to America. We must break this cycle.

Businesses can choose to follow the talent, but the universities that make up most of the research community do not have the same flexibility. "Over half of my students are permanent residents or citizens because NSF puts a lot of pressure on centers to fund U.S. students, but I'm not seeing the same range of students that I used to," says my sister Deborah Estrin, a UCLA professor of computer science. It's good that the NSF is encouraging the development of American talent, but it will take at least a generation to rebuild the talent pool, once we begin to address the education and cultural issues that are limiting the availability of scientists.

For universities and science-driven businesses, immigration is an area where government can have an immediate positive influence. "The problem continues to be cast as if industry wants to bring in scientists and engineers from overseas because they can be paid less, and that is simply ridiculous," says Symyx chairman Steve Goldby. It's not about undercutting American scientists; it's about hiring the best people.

The answer is to actively encourage immigration by providing visas and stability for highly skilled workers, while working to create the right balance of native and foreign-born employees. "We might want to become more energy efficient, but we can't cut off importation of oil, and we similarly are shooting ourselves in the foot by not welcoming foreign talent," says Deborah Estrin. "It's incredibly arrogant and just wrong to think there is not someplace else for them to go." This is a relatively easy problem to solve. We need to significantly increase or remove the caps on vetted knowledge workers who are in demand. But for political reasons, the issue of H-1B visa allocation has been attached to illegal immigration reform. They are very different issues and should be addressed separately.

INTENDED AND UNINTENDED CONSEQUENCES

Legislation, regulation, and funding that are intended to have a positive influence on organizational behavior are often accompanied by serious unintended consequences. Overregulation and litigation are running wild, discouraging businesses from taking calculated risks.

"There have been trigger points in the United States that have led to the knee-jerk reaction to regulate," says Laura Ipsen, senior VP of global policy and government affairs for Cisco. "If you ask almost any policy maker in Washington today if we overreached with the Sarbanes-Oxley Act and slowed down innovation, they will agree." When evaluating policies like SOX, we need to view them in light of their effects on innovation. We need policies that encourage risk and patience, not rules that impose metrics in the name of accountability at the expense of openness and sharing. Policy also needs to be reflective of the broad changes that are now occurring in society, like the increasing importance of smaller companies, the Internet, and personalized medicine.

Federal funding of education and R&D has the most direct impact on the Ecosystem. Tax policy and direct subsidies can influence innovation by encouraging investment that can help new ideas take root, but they can also simply reinforce the status quo if they are not carefully applied.

Providing incentives for investment, such as the corporate R&D tax credit or the capital gains tax, encourages risk taking and patience. But temporary incentives are not effective in influencing long-term behavior. Executives making decisions about where to locate R&D projects that will span multiple years need to know how to factor in the tax impact. In December of 2006, President Bush signed legislation strengthening the R&D tax credit and extending it through December 31, 2007—the thirteenth time in its 25-year history that it was given a temporary extension. The tax credit is important to encourage companies to locate R&D centers in the United States, and it should be made permanent. But the credit may not be enough to offset the level of benefits currently provided by foreign governments to corporations and individuals. A 2004 PCAST report on competitiveness cited a major U.S. semiconductor manufacturer that had found an effective $1.3 billion tax differential offered by an Asian country on a total investment of $3 billion for a major new plant.

Not all incentives for shoring up R&D in the United States need to be tax-related. One of the most significant factors in deciding where to locate an R&D center is a strong research community and talent base. As companies have been pressured to spend less on research, R&D has turned into mostly D. We should give corporations additional incentives to invest in real research, either directly or through contributions to universities. "You can either take the approach that these companies can't afford to do research—in which case they can't—or try to encourage them to do it," says VC Michael Sheridan.

The long-term capital gains tax is somewhat of a misnomer, given that it encourages holding investments for only one year. If we had a graduated capital gains tax that provided incremental benefits for those who hold stocks longer, we could encourage people to be *real* long-term investors who think in terms of years rather than months. "I would do everything I can to encourage people to have a six- to ten-year view of things," says investor Kevin Compton. The capital gains tax is up for review in 2009, and it should be extended and enhanced to encourage strategic risk taking and longer-term ownership.

The country's patent system was created to promote progress by protecting inventors' intellectual property, but nearly everyone now agrees that it is in need of reform. Beginning in the late 1990s, the money spent annually on patent litigation by publicly traded companies exceeded the profits they earned from the patents they have. Significant changes in the existing system will have to be made to mitigate the tensions between different industries, as well as a new breed of "patent trolls" that have made a business out of buying patents on spec, rather than using them to further innovation.

Industries with high up-front R&D costs, including biotech, are highly dependent on a well-functioning patent system. In the IT industry, the product life cycle is so short that patents do not provide much benefit beyond the defense of intellectual property. As a result, some major companies now see patents as adverse to their business, and are seeking changes that will make it more difficult for broad patents to be issued. "It's an incredible double whammy," says Cisco general counsel Mark Chandler. "People have patents that are worthless from an industrial standpoint, and they sell them off to entities that don't really have any inventive activity worthy of protection. These patents are then being used for lawsuits, taking advantage of rules that create outsized damage awards."

An increasing percentage of job creation and innovation comes from smaller companies. Yet we often do not think of the relative burden on them when enacting policy. As reform is underway, we need to make sure that the rights and incentives of small and medium-sized firms that don't have the same lobbying power as large corporations are taken into account.

MOON SHOT POLICY

The success of each of the four "moon shots" that I described will require funding and policy to guide investment and behavioral change in all three communities of the Ecosystem.

The American health-care system is currently neither affordable by nor accessible to many people. Medical expenditures in the United States nearly tripled from 1990 to 2005, reaching $2 trillion, and are projected to double again by 2015. This spending accounted for 16 percent of the nation's GDP, compared to approximately 10 percent of GDP in Switzerland, Germany, and Canada. Since 2001, employer-sponsored health coverage premiums have increased by 68 percent. These escalating costs burden both individuals and businesses, and they have led to an alarming rise in the number of uninsured Americans. More than one in ten U.S. citizens did not have health insurance in

2006, including nine million children under the age of 18. Solving these problems without slowing down important advances in medicine is one of the more complex policy challenges that we face. "The health-care economists say that new technology is the biggest driving force of the increase in costs in medicine," says Stanford's Paul Yock. "I think we're headed for a chill in innovation."

The information technology industry went through its own period of rapid advances, when enterprises would buy anything new. Some of this technology turned out to be superfluous, and eventually businesses figured out where IT could really help productivity and where it was a waste. The quickening pace of change in medicine has created a similar scenario. But with the complex set of agencies, businesses, nonprofits, and medical professionals that make up the country's health-care delivery system, decisions are too often motivated by profits and politics, leading us to under- or overreact. We need a system in which trust is placed in the medical professionals who understand the science and their individual patients, not one that is driven by administrators and metrics.

Innovation alone has not created the rise in costs; 7 percent of each health-care dollar spent in the United States goes to administrative costs. We should also be looking at overhead, overregulation, and excessive litigation as areas where we can reduce the financial burden. The availability of medical information (correct and incorrect) on the Internet and direct-to-consumer advertising about these advances can lead to both overtesting and overprescribing of medication. Electronic patient records have the potential to enhance the experience and quality of patient care and reduce costs long term, if they are implemented securely and in a way that works for patients and individual physicians as well as large organizations. "The federal government has really neglected its responsibility and opportunity to set any kind of framework for the development of electronic medical records," says Abby Josephs, a program manager at Stanford Hospital. "What you have is a number of different organizations putting literally billions of dollars into IT systems that cannot communicate with one another."

The Health Insurance Portability and Accountability Act (HIPAA), enacted in 1996, was intended to ensure continuity of health coverage for workers and their families when they have a change in employment. But the additional paperwork and administrative overhead created for companies, physicians, hospitals, and patients overshadowed the benefits. "It has gotten to the point where people are hiding behind HIPAA as a reason not to make changes," says Josephs. "It has led to less sharing of information, including with the patients themselves." We have to be more careful and apply all of the fundamentals of innovation to this complex problem, beginning with acknowledging that there is a diverse set of needs that must be met. The health of our children and of the economy are at stake.

The potential for disastrous unintended consequences in the areas of energy and environmental policy is enormous given the pressure put on politicians by special interest groups. Taking public stands in favor of ethanol and pushing for the growth of more corn may demonstrate a will to action, but ethanol may not be the right answer for our future energy requirements.

We need to encourage appropriate behavioral changes in the application community to conserve energy and use less petroleum-based fuel. We should accelerate the development of more energy-efficient products as well as viable alternative sources, such as solar and wind power. But we must also find new long-term solutions, which can come only from research, as well as patience and a real commitment to the future. Yet yearly government spending on energy R&D is significantly less now than it was in 1979.

As we reevaluate existing policies and develop new ones, we need to take the time to understand the trade-offs we will need to make if we are to be successful in each of the four moon shots.

RESEARCH—STRENGTHENING THE ROOTS

Our national research community is suffering from neglect. Its contributions to the products we use, the medicines we take, and the foods we eat have been nearly forgotten. Investment has been decreasing and horizons shortening as requirements and competition have increased. The Organisation for Economic Cooperation and Development recently ranked the United States twenty-second in the percentage of GDP devoted to non-defense research. For the first time, the most powerful particle accelerator in the world—which enables scientists to push the frontiers of physics and cosmology—is located in Switzerland rather than the United States. To rebuild the foundation for our future, we need to increase investment and adapt the allocation and sources of funding. We also need new models of collaboration to bring the resources of the nation to bear on the opportunities that lie ahead.

In today's culture of instant gratification, anything that is not seen as being directly connected to short-term gain is viewed as highly discretionary at best, if not an outright waste. Developing a research discovery into a commercial application can take decades, and the damage caused by underinvestment often is not visible until it's too late.

Vannevar Bush defined the distinction between basic and applied research to focus attention on the need for funding a pure quest for understanding. More than 50 years ago, he wrote: "Basic research is a long-term process—it ceases to be basic if immediate results are expected." It's easy to see why the popular view would be to push for research that is "useful" (applied) rather than searching for knowledge that does not consider its immediate practical employment (basic). We can no longer afford to view the choice in such binary terms. Our vocabulary for describing and funding research should be expanded to include work that is motivated by a quest for fundamental understanding, but with a consideration of use. The late Donald Stokes, a professor of politics and public affairs at Princeton, dubbed this type of use-inspired basic research "Pasteur's Quadrant," because many of the French microbiologist's discoveries (including what we now call pasteurization) fell into this category. If you look back at the early work funded by ARPA in the 1960s and 1970s—which led to the ways that we interact with computers and the Internet today—it consisted of basic research driven by a broad vision of potential use. Each of the four moon shots involves a set of problems that should guide both applied and use-inspired basic research.

In applied research, the targeted application is used to direct and constrain the scope of the work. Use-inspired basic research is guided by a combination of the practical and the theoretical. Potential applications that might be 5, 10, or 30 years away provide an overall context that is significantly broader than that of applied research. Probing the ways in which the brain processes information with the goal of understanding how children learn, studying genes to discover how we can treat neurodegenerative diseases like Alzheimer's or Parkinson's, and exploring alternative sources of energy are all examples of research conducted with the consideration of use. With a context of potential use, it's easier for people to understand and support the need for the kind of research that falls into Pasteur's Quadrant. But there is also a place for pure exploratory basic research. When funding agencies, either government or philanthropic, move beyond providing support for scientists to actively managing projects through tight constraints or specific deliverables, the potential of open-ended research can be dramatically limited. The country needs to invest in the full spectrum.

Most funding for basic research must come from the government, for such work is a critical part of the infrastructure of society that does not bring direct returns to any single party. "When people tell you that it doesn't pay to do research, what they are telling you is that the private rate of return is very low," says economist Paul Romer. "And that's often true—particularly for the very abstract, early-stage, unguided kind of research. But it could still be the case that the social rate of return from that research is very high."

The nature of scientific research is evolving, becoming increasingly interdisciplinary as more and more complex problems require contributions from multiple fields. A gastroenterologist and a researcher of satellite technology might work together to develop a tiny capsule containing a camera that is guided by remote control, replacing the need for more cumbersome diagnostic tools. Many of tomorrow's breakthroughs will occur at the intersections of diverse disciplines. These will not be limited only to science, engineering, and medicine, but will also include the social sciences, arts, and humanities.

Two of the most promising areas of science are concerned with the ultra-small—where biotech, IT, and nanotechnology come together—and the ultra-large, such as the study of energy systems, the environment, and health-care delivery. Even more opportunities lie where these frontiers intersect. The development of biofuels and bio-based design are prime examples of fields in which the new small-scale science may help solve large problems. As science has become more and more specialized in recent years, the challenge is to create bridges between disciplines. "Innovation happens in the cross-connections that you can't even predict," says VC Yogen Dalal. Sustainable innovation will depend on encouraging cooperation between experts in many different fields.

Launched a decade ago, Stanford's Bio-X program was the university's first experiment in interdisciplinary bioscience. Researchers from multiple departments work side by side in a new building designed specifically to facilitate collaboration. The university launched new initiatives to support this work, including a fund offering seed grants to teams containing at least two faculty members from departments at the university that hadn't collaborated before. For one project, a physicist partnered with an ear specialist to learn more about deafness. They developed a new kind of microscope that lets doctors see the hair cells in the ear more clearly, enabling them to adjust cochlear implants according to the specific needs of the patient. The project is expanding with additional funding from industry and a grant from the Wallace H. Coulter Foundation. Federal funding for Bio-X-initiated research is now ten times the amount of the initial grants given by the university. Stanford has implemented this same strategy of seed financing in its other interdisciplinary initiatives.

WHERE IS ALL THE FEDERAL MONEY GOING?

Federal research spending in science and engineering grew from over $28 billion in 1995 to over $54 billion in 2004, almost doubling in a decade. So what's the problem? The investment strategy was overly influenced by the "hot" research areas of the time, at the expense of maintaining critical mass across all areas of science. It's interesting to compare the budget increases in a few of the individual fields during that nine-year period. Life sciences increased 150 percent, to almost $30 billion. Mathematics and computer science grew 79 percent, to $2.8 billion. Investment in all areas of engineering grew 60 percent, to $9 billion. But environmental and physical sciences had increases of only 37 and 25 percent, respectively.

In other words, investment in life science research grew more than four times as fast as the investment in environmental sciences, and almost six times faster than investment in the physical sciences. There's no question that the investments in the future of IT and medical care were critical, but several of the problems that we face today—including climate change and the need for sustainable sources of energy—require expertise in engineering and the environmental and physical sciences, and these fields have been shortchanged for two decades. Discoveries in the physical sciences and IT also contribute to advances in medicine and the other life sciences. "Many of the surgical innovations in use today, like miniature cameras and advanced materials, originally came from NASA," says Stanford Hospital CEO Martha Marsh. "Physicians see these things and say, 'I could use that.'"

Because research has a delayed impact, we need to fund all key areas of science, despite the fact that it's tougher politically to justify funding in areas that most voters can't directly correlate to their daily lives. "We are eating our seed corn from the last several decades of research. You can do that for a while because there were a lot of seeds planted, but after a while they stop coming up," says Stanford's engineering dean, Jim Plummer. The NSF's 2008 Science and Engineering Indicators report brought more bad news: a 5 percent decrease in overall federal investment in research in 2007 as compared to 2004.

The increase in earmarking—funds approved by Congress or the president that are preassigned to specific projects—puts even more pressure on the budgets that are available for long-term research. Instead of trusting the experts, politicians are deciding what should be funded on the basis of their own agendas. "I have gone through lists where the leadership has said that we need to find projects in districts where there are no universities. There aren't even any companies beyond very small ones. They have to find a way to spend money there, and it's just purely the political process," says Michael Sheridan, who worked with the NSF's Small Business Innovation Research Program funding committee. We should be reinforcing our centers of excellence, not weakening them. If and when there are more funds available, we can start building additional ones. Of the $143 billion of federal R&D investment for 2008, more than $4 billion was preallocated through over four thousand earmarks.

Making funding decisions based on politics also costs us more in the end. NASA is willing to build the next high-profile $5 billion land-based telescope, but not $50 million ones—despite the fact that, according to astrophysicist Jeremiah Ostriker, you are always better off combining the data collected from multiple smaller telescopes. "Why won't NASA do it?" he asks. "It's bragging rights. It makes some congressman happy that a team is building a big project in his home district. This pushes people toward large-scale projects even when there are no economies of scale. The increasing scale of projects at all levels is crowding out the smaller ones." This costs us not only in dollars, but also in innovation. As projects get bigger, it becomes more expensive to experiment, and you are forced to narrow the scope of your research at an earlier stage.

Many in the research community have expressed concern about what's happening at DARPA, given the central role that the organization has played in sustaining our Innovation Ecosystem in the past. Under the agency's current administration, there's even less freedom for individual researchers to explore areas that might not necessarily fit a specific military R&D program. DARPA has become more programmatic, funding only research that promises some immediate outcome, and structuring its programs with short-term deliverables. "Tony

Tether has the view that any proposal has to have numerical, quantifiable metrics to indicate whether you're accomplishing your goal," says researcher Dave Clark. This discourages the higher-risk, longer-term projects that we so desperately need.

An increasing amount of research is classified, sometimes for opaque reasons, which may even work *against* national security. "The classification leads to a disconnect with the university community," explains David Tennenhouse, who was an office director at DARPA in the late 1990s. "If we needed to work with university researchers in a hurry, we knew who they were, and we had the ability to act quickly on issues, tapping into the best minds in the country. Classification also has an impact on quality. The last time I looked at what DARPA was funding, some of it wasn't really new, and there was stuff that was outright screwy. It didn't look like science." Overclassification has eroded the agency's relationship with top-tier innovators, to the detriment of the research community and our country. Instead of nourishing the national Ecosystem, DARPA-funded projects have become more like a corporate research arm of the Pentagon.

The National Science Foundation has a very broad mission as the only agency that is focused on supporting science and engineering in virtually every discipline. But its budget is not sufficient to compensate for the changes at DARPA, and with the scarcity of funds, NSF grants are generally too small to support cutting-edge, high-risk, high-return research. "There's an attitude of spreading the wealth and making grants that enable you to get another grant, as opposed to actually succeeding at what you've proposed," says chemist Richard Zare. Researchers have to spend too much time fund-raising and worrying about money, which interferes with their work.

The NSF uses a peer review process that tends to reinforce the status quo, weeding out proposals that are nonmainstream, like the kinds of projects that led to the modern era of computing. "It's very hard for an NSF-style review panel to select things that are really on the edge, because they're almost certain to offend somebody on the panel," says Tennenhouse. A researcher working in an area of highly disruptive innovation may have no real "peers." Scientific communities, like many communities, gravitate toward the predominant school of thought, and outliers suffer. "Peer review has a definite role, but farther down in the process," says Robert Spinrad, who served in advisory roles for both DARPA and the NSF. "The grant process also has to include mechanisms to fund wildly imaginative excursions."

The competition for contracts has gotten stiffer. Eligible universities used to number in the hundreds; now there are thousands. "You've got more people trying to eat from a pie that's not getting bigger," explains National Academy of Engineering president Charles Vest. "If you're trying to figure out how to wisely administer grants at NSF or NIH, you have to think about how you keep creating opportunity for new people when you hardly have enough money to keep the solid people moving forward."

Not only is the current rate of government research funding too low, but it's too volatile. Multiyear projects require consistency in the funding base. The doubling of the National Institutes of Health budget in the five years after 1998 was a good investment. But after 2003, the total amount actually went down relative to inflation. "When this doubling happened, every provost in the country started building labs, making plans, and telling senior researchers that instead of having one or two grants, they had to have two or three," says Daniel Goroff, professor of mathematics and economics at Harvey Mudd College. "Now that it's leveled off, they're all looking at each other and wondering what to do."

As a child, I felt the tensions of the funding process even without knowing what a grant was. When one of my parents was preparing to apply for a grant, we knew to be good and give them space. As my father recalls, "It was always a very tense time. Our ability to continue our work was in the hands of a process that was time consuming and somewhat arbitrary, and I knew that my researchers were dependent on the funding for their livelihood." The research community has always felt the pressure of scarcity, but my parents had to go through the process only every couple of years—nothing like today.

As we increase overall funding for research, we need to focus on encouraging young researchers, fostering interdisciplinary programs, and bringing back our appetite for risk. As important as the discoveries that come from the research community are the students who carry these new ideas out into the Ecosystem. "One of the reasons you'd like to maintain a vibrant research activity infrastructure in your economy is because it trains people who become valuable assets for a nation to have," says economist Paul Romer. "Training really talented people is like having a lot of fuel around. You never know where this human fuel is going to spark something."

When a field is funded below a certain level, this discourages new students. Thus not only have we missed an opportunity in research, we have lost a generation of talent. We should have more graduate fellowships that go to directly to top students, enabling them to choose where they think they'll have the best educational experience. The better public and private universities will go out of their way to attract these bright kids, fostering competition. In the 1960s and the 1970s, fellowships from the National Defense Education Act and the DOD provided a foundation of research for the whole country. But we must also continue to invest in the experienced faculty and researchers who mentor these students and young staff, informing their fresh ideas with an understanding of the art of science.

As we train the next generation of researchers, we need to make room for new collaborative models—without forgetting that strong interdisciplinary work can't happen without sturdy research foundations in the individual fields themselves. My sister's multidisciplinary program, the Center for Embedded Networked Sensing (CENS), brings people with skill sets in environmental engineering, seismology, and marine ecosystems together with those in image processing, signal processing, and statistics. CENS is funded through the NSF's Science Technology Center Program. "It's not just an umbrella grant to a few institutions," Deborah explains. "The idea is that you fund a collection of research that couldn't happen independently through a larger number of smaller grants." CENS received a funding commitment of $40 million over a ten-year period, which will enable a broad spectrum of research. These larger, long-term NSF grants are critical to filling the hole left by DARPA, and we need more of them. The NIH has also added research program grants requiring interdisciplinary connections.

The country must increase its overall commitment to basic science. The additional dollars required to make a big difference in research are minuscule compared to the overall federal budget. "The NSF spent $181 million in 2006 in all of chemistry, and about $200 million in land-based astronomy. And the operational cost of the war in Iraq is something like $300 million a day," says scientist Richard Zare.

At our current rate of investment, we will end up having to leverage research in other countries while shortening the innovation horizon in the United States. This is not a viable strategy for success. There is a tight link in the nation's universities between research and education. Whether students who are taught and trained by great researchers stay in academia or work in industry, they have learned how to think and how to innovate. We must not become strategically dependent on other countries in a way that makes us weak. Only from a position of strength will we be open to the collaboration necessary to face the challenges and opportunities ahead of us. We cannot assume that the information flow between China and the United States will be as open and efficient as the flow between Los Angeles and Boston. Changes in world affairs could cut off our ability to import innovation without warning.

It is only through our own research efforts that we will have the expertise to evaluate, import, and build on discoveries made elsewhere. "The Japanese or Koreans were able to take advantage of the technology all over the world because they had the educational base to do it," says scientist Jeremiah Ostriker. "If the United States does not have the research labs that can take advantage of things done elsewhere, then it will not do it. We will become the Third World."

VISIONARY GIVING

Philanthropic foundations and individuals have always played an important role in the research community through gifts to academic institutions and specific research grants. Some organizations have particularly distinguished themselves by their strong commitments to basic research and long-term horizons. The Howard Hughes Medical Institute (HHMI) was launched in 1953 with the mission of probing "the genesis of life itself," in the words of its reclusive founder. Today the institute is a leader in biomedical research. "The HHMI has a really thoughtful attitude about identifying exceptional scientists and effectively giving them funding for renewable periods of five years," says GNF director Peter Schultz. "They ask retrospectively what has been accomplished. If the grantees have done good things, they give them another five years of funding."

The MacArthur Foundation—also 30 years old, with more than $6 billion in assets—is one of the country's largest private philanthropic institutions. Its mission is to foster lasting improvement in the human condition through grants and fellowships. The foundation also supports a set of interdisciplinary networks, which it calls "research institutions without walls," that bring together highly talented individuals from a spectrum of disciplines, perspectives, and research methods. One member of the foundation's Mind-Body Network, Esther Sternberg, is internationally recognized for her discoveries in brain-immune interactions and the effects of stress on health, and currently works at the National Institute of Mental Health. "The network started out as a small group of very cutting-edge, risk-taking scientists who were all feeling ostracized by the prevailing dogmas in their institutions and fields," she says. "But we would get together three times a year, and it was like being a camel in the desert. We'd drink up this water of support, which gave us the courage to go back and continue, knowing that what we were doing was risky, but also rigorous and real."

Though the Internet bubble had many negative effects on the Innovation Ecosystem, there may be a silver lining. Over the next decade, money from what VC John Doerr called "the greatest legal creation of wealth in history" will flow into philanthropy, resulting in foundations started by technologists and entrepreneurs who are used to making things happen. This new generation of funding organizations, including the Bill & Melinda Gates Foundation, has the potential to bring a new level of focus and strategic thinking to philanthropy. "An unbelievable number of foundations with huge amounts of money have been created by people who were innovators," says investor Roger McNamee.

While these foundations do a lot of good, their efforts tend to be focused primarily on the application community. Many Internet entrepreneurs do not have the patience to fund long-term research. "People take to their philanthropy the same mindset that they used in their business activities, and it tends to be short-term," says Computer History Museum founder Len Shustek. Considering that the fortunes of these entrepreneurs were built on research funded 30 years ago, they should commit some of their efforts to investing in long-range projects. Just 10 percent of these foundations' wealth could go a long way toward leveraging government funding in research.

Smaller foundations that are willing to collaborate amplify their resources. Actor Michael J. Fox and former Intel CEO Andy Grove—both of whom suffer from Parkinson's disease—launched foundations in 2000 with the goal of accelerating the pace of scientific research in and improving therapy for the disorder. The Michael J. Fox Foundation is a public charity with a portfolio approach, emphasizing a broad research agenda. Grove's Kinetics Foundation, which is private, reflects its founder's laser-sharp mind and energetic personality. With a focused and decisive style, it is targeted at more applied research, identifying key areas that are not fundable through traditional mechanisms. The two foundations have built a close relationship, with each pursuing its own agenda while working together in specific areas to sponsor workshops and define problems to be solved. Between 2001 and 2006, when the funding for stem-cell research was most threatened, they worked together to fill the gap.

The Bill & Melinda Gates Foundation's Global Health Program is committed to curing infectious diseases among the poorest of the poor in the developing world. Its focus has been primarily on the delivery of health care. But the foundation recognizes that there are not enough resources going into drug discovery and research to accomplish its mission, and it recently brought in Carol Dahl as director of Global Health Discovery.

The foundation uses a variety of methods to decide what to fund, but it is increasingly proactive, defining a set of key questions to investigate and soliciting the community so that the best players can self-identify. It uses a stepwise process of funding, starting with small seed grants. "When you're asking for extreme innovations and paradigm-shifting views, you're not necessarily looking for somebody who has done preliminary work, but you *are* looking for someone who has done preliminary thought," says Dahl. "We get people working on disparate problems toward the same endpoint and are able to have a catalytic impact that results in researchers becoming more committed to the problem, because with that collaboration comes new ideas and new creativity."

At a time when the government is so driven by partisanship and businesses are struggling to look beyond the next quarter, nonprofits may be the best positioned to think long-term. This will require the right leadership and a sufficient level of endowments to provide continuity of funding. Large foundations or partnerships of smaller ones are most effective when they have a clear vision and the resources to be like the old ARPA—funding people, not projects, and building community.

PRIZING INNOVATION

Creating audacious challenges can accelerate innovation. In the 1700s, the British Parliament offered a "longitude prize" to anyone who discovered how to pinpoint a location in the open sea. Scientific prizes and grand challenges are now becoming popular again and are playing an important role in applied research.

One of the best known of these prizes is the X Prize, created in 1996 for the first private manned space flight. In 2004, $10 million was awarded for the flight of SpaceshipOne to a team financed by Microsoft cofounder Paul Allen. The X Prize Foundation defines problems and creates challenges, awarding money for results instead of research. X Prize competitions are currently under way in genomics and fuel-efficient automobiles. The foundation also has a joint prize with Google to support a robotics race to the moon. DARPA employs a combination of up-front funding and prize money in the form of its Grand Challenges, aimed at accelerating the development of autonomous ground vehicles.

Even companies are starting to award prizes to help leverage their internal innovation. Netflix recently announced a $1 million award for the team that builds the best algorithm to predict what movie a customer might like to watch based on his or her rental history. To win, the system must be at least 10 percent better than the company's current approach. Talented people immediately started downloading the database that Netflix made available. The competition will go on for five years, with Netflix posting updates on its Web site to add peer recognition to the incentive.

The advantage of prizes is that you pay only for performance, and anyone can compete. The winner of the longitude prize was not an astronomer but a clockmaker. Successful prizes frame the right questions and define problems that are worthy and exciting. But the very strength of awards like this—that they provide a narrow and clear focus for research—can also be their downside. The researchers may end up missing out on learning that doesn't contribute directly to the goal. Prizes should not be substituted for grants; they should augment them and help boost popular excitement about science and technology.

HOME TO THE RESEARCH COMMUNITY

The research community used to be distributed among industry, government labs, and universities. Now it has been consolidated primarily in academia. Not only are universities the best places to conduct long-term research, but participating in research is an important part of training for the next generation of innovators. And working with students keeps the faculty young.

As academic institutions and communities assume more responsibility for furthering research, it is all the more critical that they embrace innovation's core values. Competition for funds and tenure hardens the walls between university departments and schools and encourages shorter-term incremental research, instead of rewarding collaboration and risk. Patience and openness are strained as an increase in industry funding and the rise of licensing offices has pushed faculty and students toward early commercialization, often at the expense of furthering knowledge. We need to change the ways in which young researchers are mentored and measured to bring out their full potential more effectively.

When Esther Sternberg began her career in the 1970s, her professors encouraged her to take risks. She remembers submitting a paper to the *New England Journal of Medicine* that was accepted immediately. The head of the rheumatology department at her university was flabbergasted and said that he hadn't thought it was going to fly. But he never discouraged her from trying and even encouraged her, despite his doubts. "It's unfortunate that kids now have to be so narrowly focused on publishing papers from the very beginning," she says. "They end up rarely doing anything that has a potential to fail." Students and young professors are tempted to choose those projects that offer the best chance of getting published quickly, rather than those that result in learning how to think. "I think academia right now is stuck in a model where the simplest way to protect your own career is to straighten up, fly right, play by the rules, and don't take risks," says MIT's Dave Clark.

For hundreds of years, universities have been organized around the notion of encouraging scholars to drill down deeply in a narrow area of expertise. The universities of the future will have more permeable walls between their departments and robust interdisciplinary programs. But to achieve this will involve significant change in academic business as usual.

Faculty members are typically anxious about advancement up the ladder and about continuity of funding for their research programs. Interdisciplinary collaborations and risky research projects can seem like a less-certain path to ensuring both. Academic evaluations are almost always based on individual contributions, and as a young faculty member, you have to prove that your work is unique. Collaborative and interdisciplinary work can blur those lines. If you are out working with other departments, teaching in other programs, and doing administrative tasks for other units, that's time not spent working or teaching for your department. "A lot of universities are working on addressing what is well recognized as a problem, but it's still deep, deep, deep in our culture to not credit people for interdisciplinary collaborations," says bioengineering professor Paul Yock. Professors can feel more secure once they have tenure, but for the first seven or eight years, the obligation to publish or perish can discourage interdisciplinary work. Changes in promotion criteria, shared physical space, seed funding, supportive mentors, and tools that help students find others who share or complement their interests can all help to counteract this trend.

RELATIONSHIPS OF IMPORTANCE

As universities assume responsibility for more research, their relationships with corporations need to become more collaborative. "We have to recognize that the *really* new, new thing—which is capable of creating a new industry—is more than likely to come from the universities these days," says John Hennessy, president of Stanford University. In order to ensure that this research eventually finds its way into the industrial sector, we need to strengthen the working relationships between academia and industry.

Industry-university relations have historically been very transactional. Corporations provide funding or equipment; universities train future employees and generate new ideas. At Stanford, Ellen Levy experimented with pushing these relationships to a more collaborative level. In trying to move the players beyond simple transactions like donations of money or licensing of ideas, she came up with what she calls her "ROI model," which is a clever way of thinking about where we need to go. She found that industry partners were always making decisions based on their *return on investment*—something that universities and government agencies don't generally focus on. "I came up with the notion that ROI, like everything else, needs to be translated," Levy explains. "In industry, 'ROI' means return on investment. But for the university, it could mean *research of interest*, and for government, it could mean *results of importance*. Each participant is driven by ROI—just not by the ROI that the others think is at work."

The trick to forging these deeper relationships between institutions and enterprises is to find a research area or problem set that maps into each one's ROI. Doing that mapping is a role for the facilitators and connectors who communicate with everyone involved. When I first heard Levy describe her model, I realized that the acronym could also be used to mean a *relationship of interaction*, transforming mere transactions into true collaborations. When all the interactions align, you get innovations like the large CCD chips that are at the heart of today's high-resolution digital cameras. "That was the result of a very close collaboration between the military, which was using those chips in satellites to look down; astronomers, who were using them to look up; and corporations, which were working with both groups to develop the chips," says astronomer Jeremiah Ostriker. "So that was a three-way partnership that was extremely effective."

As government funding for research becomes harder to get, many universities are looking to corporations for funds. "If you look at our portfolio here in the engineering school, it's much less dependent on DARPA than it used to be," says Stanford engineering dean Jim Plummer. "Faculty members at the better places have been driven to be really innovative in finding ways to do the things they want to do."

Significant corporate-sponsored research institutes have recently been created in the energy field. Businesses that rely on university research should be picking up more of the tab. But we need to be very careful that these investments do not come with strings attached that might compromise the time horizon or integrity of the research.

"The presidents, deans, and department chairmen are caught, because this is good money," says Robert Spinrad, who spent much of his career leading corporate research. "But as a result, they're also becoming too captive to the pragmatic." Especially in the area of basic research, universities need to be careful not to limit the sharing of results through early-stage patents or restrictions on what is published. These actions might seem to be in the best interest of the corporate sponsors in the short term. But they are not good for sustaining the Ecosystem, thus hurting everyone over the long term.

THE LAB GAP

As corporations shut down their R&D labs or redirected them toward shorter-term research, the Ecosystem lost a critical function: its ability to prototype ideas on a large scale without the business pressures of corporate development groups. The big corporate labs brought together a wide spectrum of people and gave them the time and scope to work on tough, long-range problems on a scale larger than universities can manage. The decline of these institutions has resulted in a *lab gap*.

The mission of universities is discovery and education. They don't have the resources or the expertise to do the rapid prototyping that is a critical step between early research and development, and start-ups don't have the money or the patience to step in and take over the job. This problem has been somewhat masked in IT by the fact that much of the recent focus is on software, consumer Web sites, security, and mobile applications—fields in which large-scale prototyping is easier, even in a university. Google is working with IBM and the NSF to set up a center for the study of large-scale computing. "When I've had people here from Berkeley, Stanford, and other places," says Google's Bill Coughran, "they've said, 'Wow, you guys are computing on a scale that I don't know how to replicate or even teach my students in the university.' We need to figure out a way to fund that, and we are trying to do what we can at our end."

In other important fields from medicine to energy, where large-scale precommercial development and experimentation is complex and expensive, you can get only so far in a small lab. "This is a huge issue in the energy and environment area, as well as the life sciences," says Stanford dean Jim Plummer. "We need labs that have the people and the physical resources to try things at a larger scale."

We should not try to recreate the past. The lab gap should be filled with a variety of collaborations between existing research organizations and universities, as well as new models of virtual research networks that enable scientists to collaborate at a distance.

In 1998, the Semiconductor Industry Association (SIA) recognized that we were suffering from a lab gap and set up a network of Focus Centers at select universities. "We needed to create a virtual Bell Labs," says SIA CEO George Scalise. Each center has a specific field of research to tackle, from advancing the state of semiconductor design and testing to exploring nanomaterials. The Focus Centers act as hubs, facilitating collaboration with researchers at universities all over the country.

Google's need for affordable, clean energy to power its data centers has led the company to create a new initiative called RE < C, which stands for "renewable energy is cheaper than coal." Google plans to invest hundreds of millions of dollars in the research, development, and application of alternative energy. If this is done in an open fashion, it could be the equivalent of Bell Labs' invention of the transistor to replace costly vacuum tubes, and it could benefit the entire Innovation Ecosystem, as well as planet Earth's.

NETWORKS OF NETWORKS

Over time, the notion of interdisciplinary research should be extended beyond the walls of a single institution to include global networks of researchers brought together by a grand challenge, such as tackling aspects of the four moon shots. The MacArthur Foundation's interdisciplinary networks provide a model that could be replicated and expanded in order to build networks of networks, analogous to the way the Internet itself was created. "It's social capital, rather than the human capital of individuals alone, that makes the big difference," says Professor Daniel Goroff of Harvey Mudd College. Funding would not be given to an individual or an institution, but to the core mission itself, with a selected organization acting as the glue by providing focus, infrastructure, and coordination for the researchers. This coordination function could be played by a government agency or some other nonprofit organization.

Using modern tools for off-site collaboration, these global research networks could be extended with virtual labs for large-scale prototyping and testing. Expensive equipment required for experimentation could be located in centers adjacent to universities, similar to the NSF supercomputing centers or the SIA's Focus Centers. Industry expertise would be needed to operate these centers and provide a commercial perspective.

The Internet was created to share computing resources. We can now also use it to share other types of scientific tools. Researchers can now use expensive electron microscopes that are shared online by controlling the equipment remotely; thus, they have access to millions of dollars of equipment, rented for an hour at a time. "You're beginning to see start-ups that are figuring out how to play in this new mixture of powerful wisdom and powerful computing," says scientist John Seely Brown, "with a very small number of people who are infinitely gifted and have deep connections back to the universities. The question in these exponential times becomes, is there a new way of doing science?"

AMERICA COMPETES—
ISN'T THE PROBLEM SOLVED?

A 2005 National Academies report called *Rising Above the Gathering Storm: Energizing and Employing America for a Brighter Economic Future* raised the profile of the problems we face as a nation. A committee of leaders from industry and academia, chaired by Norm Augustine, was asked to outline the "top 10 actions, in priority order, that federal policymakers could take to enhance the science and technology enterprise so that the United States can successfully compete, prosper, and be secure in the global community of the twenty-first century." The report's recommendations encompassed improvements in America's K-12 science and math education; strengthening our commitment to long-term basic research; making the United States the most attractive place to study and conduct research for both American and foreign-born scientists; and ensuring that the United States is the premier place to innovate by modernizing the patent system, realigning tax policies, and ensuring affordable broadband. The committee believed that all of these things will have to be in place *at a minimum* for the country to remain innovative.

In July 2007, Congress enacted legislation called the America COMPETES Act, the result of a bipartisan effort to respond to the recommendations in the National Academies report. The act included proposed increases in funding for the NSF, the National Institute of Standards and Technology, and the DOE Office of Science budgets, and it established the equivalent of DARPA for the energy problem to allocate funds to universities and companies. It authorized new grant programs aimed at enhancing education and suggested several other studies.

The bill did authorize funding—but alas, it didn't actually allocate the funds themselves. "In the past, Congress has passed legislation that says that the NSF budget should be doubled over 10 years, and then they turned around and cut it in the annual budget process," says Berkeley's Tom Kalil, who was deputy director of the White House National Economic Council during the Clinton administration. Changes in the annual appropriations process are what really make a difference, because authorization is neither necessary nor sufficient to result in increased funding for research. In fact, President Bush's 2008 budget did not have the increases authorized in the bill. Instead, funding for key science agencies was effectively kept flat or cut. We need to keep the pressure on the politicians, letting them know that the problem has not been solved.

The Department of Commerce is also investigating ways of measuring innovation. But focusing on metrics, patents, papers, or test scores will only cause us to pay attention to the wrong things or give us a false sense of comfort. What we need to measure is our commitment level. Our success will be demonstrated in economic growth, and the progress we make toward reversing global climate change, finding sustainable energy sources, restoring America's standing in the world, and making health care accessible to everyone. To accomplish these ambitious goals, we will need a well-balanced Ecosystem fueled by talented scientists, technologists, and innovators, many of whom are not yet born. Without an education system and culture that develops and inspires future generations, there is little hope of success.

CHAPTER 8

NEXT-GENERATION INNOVATORS

There is no innovation that is more important for the world than the development of young minds. The future of our economy, the fabric of our society, and the ability to achieve our goals for the four "moon shots" will all depend on how well we prepare future generations for the twenty-first-century workplace.

When our country shifted from an agricultural economy to an industrial one in the early twentieth century, emerging technologies like pesticides, the internal-combustion engine, and new crop varieties were poised to wipe out the demand for farm labor. "History should be a guide here," says economist Paul Romer. "We faced a serious threat: an agriculturally based labor force with a large percentage of jobs about to be destroyed. So how did we respond? We reduced the supply of low-skilled workers by educating them." Indeed, the federal government mandated secondary education for all and then provided funding support. We ensured that the next generation had the skills required to be productive in a new kind of economy. "Investments in education are unique," Romer explains. "It's the one policy that makes the pie bigger, because a more educated workforce leads to more output and keeps everybody sharing relatively equally in the division of the pie." Educating the labor force also provided workers with more options while making less-educated workers scarcer, thus increasing their wages.

Today, technological advances, shifts in global trade patterns, and changing demographics all pose a similar challenge, and these forces are already widening the income equality gap in the United States. College graduates earn at least 130 percent more than those who only finish high school. But one-third of our eighth graders never receive a high school diploma, and of those who do, 40 percent do not pursue a college education. And half of those who do enroll in college never earn a bachelor's degree. At the same time, there is less and less domestic demand for routine tasks that can be automated or shipped offshore. We need to revamp our educational system again, this time by changing what and how we teach.

In recent years, a lot of attention has been paid to the state of our country's K-12 educational system, but when viewed through the lens of innovation, our policy decisions, leadership structure, and funding have not been aligned for success. We are so busy administering standardized tests that we have forgotten that a test score does not always correlate with real assessment and learning. We are not making the right investments in developing new curricula and refining teaching methods. We require a better understanding of how kids learn, and more accurate tools to diagnose problems and measure true progress. We are drowning in rivers of statistics comparing test results to past performance or to scores from other countries, but we still haven't clearly identified our needs or framed the questions that we should be asking about education. We are so caught up in the numbers that we have lost our focus on teaching. It is hard to argue with the goal of having every American child graduate from college—unless trying to achieve that goal is at the expense of those who may be better suited for a different path to success.

Effecting change is not easy in a system that is distributed across 15,000 locally managed districts with highly entrenched and diverse ways of operating. "We have some of the best schools in the world, bar none, and we also have some of the poorest-performing schools," says Professor Daniel Goroff. "The way the system has evolved in the United States has led to tremendous inequities." Funding and policy come from local, state, and federal governments, and are strongly dependent on the support of the local community. The structure of the system makes it very difficult to propagate good ideas from one region to another.

This diversity can be leveraged to our advantage if we approach the problem like innovators. Once we correctly identify the nation's short- and long-term needs, we can try various approaches on a smaller scale—in one or more schools or districts—and then share and evaluate to determine the methods that should be rolled out on a broader basis. We need to operate independently but manage collaboratively so that we can compete collectively.

WHAT DO WE NEED?

The country's educational system must inspire students so that they're prepared for careers that are satisfying and financially rewarding. We need to go beyond teaching fundamentals and help all children learn how to be more creative and better at communicating, socializing, and problem solving so that they have unique skills to offer in tomorrow's workplace. We also need to help them develop into productive members of society, ready to raise their own children with the ability to think critically and make good decisions.

We should not be in denial regarding the level and number of jobs that have moved to other countries or have been replaced by technology. Those jobs are gone. But there are still opportunities for those with the right skills. It is no longer sufficient to focus solely on training "knowledge workers," a term coined by Peter Drucker in 1959 to describe people who work primarily with information or who develop and use knowledge in the workplace. In a world in which information and technology have permeated all aspects of our lives, all workers are essentially knowledge workers, and their jobs are no longer protected from moving offshore. We need to prepare a workforce of innovators who will be employed in the creation of new markets, products, and services, as well as in jobs that require a human touch. All will require a base level of understanding of technology in the workplace and at home.

Much of the discussion of education reform today focuses specifically on math and science education, which is in great need of improvement. These also happen to be subjects that appear to be easily testable, with multiple-choice questions yielding quantifiable benchmarks. But we also have to educate our kids to think outside the box—or outside the bubble on the testing sheet. We will certainly need more well-trained scientists, mathematicians, and engineers to fuel the Innovation Ecosystem, but the reach of the Ecosystem extends beyond math, science, and engineering into the arts and humanities, as well as other vocations.

We will need talented people in business, design, operations, and administration to bring new products to market. We will need companies and individuals who know how to apply technology in creative ways, as well as savvy small business owners, lawyers, economists, political leaders, and journalists. All of these jobs will require better education and a higher level of collaboration and adaptability than ever before.

Our national infrastructure—from bridges to highways to our cities themselves—has suffered as much decline in recent years as the Innovation Ecosystem. To restore them both will call upon the efforts and passion of visionary engineers, architects, and construction workers with comprehensive knowledge of "green building" design, as well as well-trained technicians and repair crews who keep everything running.

The Internet created unforeseen opportunities for people who learned how to install and operate the new data networks. Advances in medical imaging created jobs for new types of technicians. Embracing sources of alternative energy will create similar opportunities for those who learn how to evaluate, install, and fix new products, from solar panels to electric cars.

Skilled artists, writers, and musicians will never find their jobs suddenly offshored. These professions have been transformed by the digital revolution and the advent of user-created media, and future generations of innovators in these fields will need the ability to understand and leverage new technology and adapt to changing business models.

Most of all, we will need superb teachers to inspire and inform the next generation, guiding our children to recognize their own unique gifts while learning the skills required to excel. We need to ensure that our educational system supports these teachers, while remaining flexible enough to meet changing market demand in the evolving workforce.

As citizens, we need to become more informed about the issues affecting our lives. Many Americans are unable to evaluate public policy issues critically and make the right choices for themselves and for the country. In a 2006 NSF survey, more than a third of the adult population didn't know that the Earth revolves around the sun, and more than half were unaware that antibiotics kill only bacteria and not viruses. To live and work effectively in today's world requires a basic level of scientific and technological understanding that exceeds what was required in past generations. "Citizens need to be information literate," says

VC John Doerr. "You need to be able to read and write, but you also need the ability to manipulate symbols in the broadest sense." We cannot explicitly teach people to make good decisions, but we can enhance their ability to ask the right questions, listen, and evaluate.

The overriding need in education now is not increasing third-grade test scores, but preparing our children for their work and lives in the future. This is not just the responsibility of our educational system, but also of parents, the country's leaders, the media, and every individual who influences the culture in which we live.

FOUR QUESTIONS ABOUT THE
FUTURE OF EDUCATION

These needs will not be met by solving one overarching problem. If we want the country to be capable of sustainable innovation, there are several questions that need to be addressed.

How do we ensure a solid broad-based education for all Americans, so that they're prepared to enter the workplace as contributing members of society?

If we don't face up to our need to transform education, America will have massive numbers of people who are unprepared to play meaningful roles in the twenty-first-century economy. In large urban areas, significant numbers of kids who never graduated from high school are finding their options increasingly limited. The burden on our society of a perpetually underemployed underclass will be enormous. "We have a racial and ethnic achievement gap that is staggering in its dimensions and that is being exacerbated by global achievement gaps," says Joel Klein, chancellor of New York City's Department of Education. Americans are used to seeing other regions of the world where lack of employment opportunities has led to destabilization, but they rarely imagine that the same thing could happen here at home.

Many schools are taking on more responsibilities without a sufficient increase in budgets to support them. Kids don't learn well if they can't afford to eat, so schools provide hot breakfast and lunch. The schools also have to deal with discipline problems that are unfortunately not being addressed at home. Demographic shifts in some states have led to teaching in multiple languages. With learning disabilities on the rise, schools need to invest in special education programs. Although we spend more money per student than most countries in the world, we still fall short, canceling art classes and field trips, or anything else that is not considered mandatory. But these things are mandatory for inspiring and developing future innovators.

What changes can we make to increase the level of scientific literacy?

Work and personal life these days require being able to use a computer, the Internet, and cell phones. As individuals, making well-informed decisions about personal health, saving energy, and reducing carbon emissions depends upon having a knowledge of basic math and science. At the corporate level, there is a need for people who know how to leverage information technology, but we also need people with other scientific skills, such as the expertise to evaluate the environmental impacts of their businesses. For the nation, maintaining a healthy democracy depends on the voting public being informed about issues of importance and possessing a basic knowledge of science and technology.

How can we identify, inspire, and develop students who have the aptitude to excel in science, math, or engineering?

With all that we have to do to provide basic education, it's easy to lose sight of the high achievers. We need a system that educates all children to a basic standard, but also invests in those who will become the scientists, engineers, technologists, and leaders of the future. These are the people who directly and indirectly create many of the jobs for the rest of the population. We must encourage them and enable them to fulfill their potential.

An education in math or science provides a foundation for many professions outside of science and engineering. We need entrepreneurs, businesspeople, teachers, lawyers, and politicians who have a deeper understanding of these fields. As Carl Sagan said, "Science is a way of thinking much more than it is a body of knowledge."

Young kids start out excited by science because they are naturally curious. But the longer they stay in school, the less interested they become. "If you look at 15-year-olds, their abiding interest in life is biology, and yet biology is taught in such a way that no one has the slightest interest in it," says Symyx's Steve Goldby. Today far fewer high school and college students are actively involved in science or engineering than in previous eras.

How do we increase the interest level in science and engineering among girls and women so that we can leverage the country's full talent pool?

I never questioned whether women belonged in the world of technology, in part because my mother was an engineer. As I moved through school and into the workplace, I became accustomed to being the only woman in rooms filled with men. But during that time, there has been a shift in the reason why women are in the minority in these fields, from a demand-side problem to one of supply.

Many girls decide not to take the necessary classes earlier in their education, and then don't have the option of going into science or engineering in college. "We have found that starting in fifth or sixth grade, girls start to drift away from science. In both the school system and the culture, we start to knock it out of them," says former astronaut Sally Ride. While the professional obstacles that women face in the workplace are fewer than they were, societal pressures still exert a chilling effect on girls' interest in science. "Every 11-year-old girl is told that she can be whatever she wants to be, but society is telling her something very different," Ride observes. Even female students who do well in math and science through high school often choose to pursue other careers. They want to interact with people; they want to make a difference in the world—but they don't have a clear understanding that you can achieve both with a career in science or engineering, because we haven't depicted it for them.

To find the best answers to these questions, we will need to try a variety of approaches, ensuring that we collect the right data to assess and adapt while not stifling learning by applying metrics of questionable value. The answers will depend on leadership from parents, legislators, principals, superintendents, and local school boards. But most of all, they will require great teachers.

A RESPECTED PROFESSION

Leadership is the catalyst of innovation throughout the Ecosystem, and that's particularly true in the classroom. But it's hard to attract high achievers to teaching when the profession is not given the respect or compensation that it deserves.

The roots of this problem go all the way back to the days when teaching was one of the very few careers open to women. Smart, ambitious female teachers inspired generations of students in the classroom. At the same time, however, enduring precedents were set for paying teachers less than they deserve because women were not viewed as primary breadwinners. "There weren't any other opportunities, and so that's what women did for relatively low pay. It was such a gift to teaching," says eBay's Meg Whitman. Today, many of those potentially great teachers elect instead to become bankers, lawyers, and CEOs. As opportunities for women have opened up in other fields, we have not significantly updated the way we reward teachers, making it hard to compete for talent.

In 2004, the average annual starting salary for a teacher in the United States was less than $32,000—that's $10,000 less than the average salary for college graduates who major in anything *but* education. And the numbers do not get better for experienced teachers. The U.S. Bureau of Labor Statistics lists the mean annual salary of elementary school teachers as $48,000 and that of secondary school teachers as $51,000, roughly the same pay scale as subway conductors. According to the NSF, the average salary for high school math and science teachers in 2003 was $43,000—up less than 8 percent from a decade earlier, despite a much higher increase in the cost of living. (By contrast, salaries for computer system analysts, accountants, and engineers were in the range of $60,000 to $75,000, reflecting a 20 percent increase over the same time period.) We are not providing the financial and career incentives to attract and retain highly talented teachers.

With pay scales like this, we have turned educating our children into the equivalent of an entry-level job that people do for a few years. Fixing the problem will require boosting starting salaries and making sure that there is a way for truly extraordinary teachers to be paid competitively throughout their careers. They also should be recognized for their accomplishments in the community—by reaching out to parents or mentoring other teachers—as well as in the classroom.

The notion of paying teachers on the basis of performance is a challenging one. Pegging pay scales to students' scores on standardized tests would be a terrible mistake. Teachers should not be penalized for working with disadvantaged students, who typically do not show adequate yearly progress, or implicitly encouraged to fight over students who excel academically. Our kids do not need to feel any more pressure about standardized tests.

We also need to be able to identify inadequate or merely mediocre teachers more effectively. The compensation structure needs to be transformed to bring more flexibility and discretion into the system. To do this will require strong leadership on the part of school administrations. "The unions have got to be partners in this transformation. The assembly-line view of worker compensation can't work, and we should be candid about that," says education chancellor Joel Klein. "The question is, how do we transform teachers' unions into professional organizations that believe employment should be built on meritocracy? In the words of a 24-year-old I know, 'What kind of system is it in which whether you work hard or don't work hard, do well or don't, you get paid the same unless you stay another year, in which case you get paid a little more?' We've got to transform that paradigm."

It's easy to target costly pension plans and an outdated tenure system as potential areas for change, but they need to be viewed in the context of an overall compensation package that balances salary, benefits, and job security. Once we determine the right long-term approach, we will need a transition strategy that takes care of those who have committed their lives to the service of our children.

Graduate programs in education focus mostly on pedagogy. Teachers in training need to form partnerships with experts in other disciplines to ensure that as they learn how to teach, they're also digging deeply into the subjects they'll be teaching, beyond a basic level. For example, the Harvard Extension School offers a master's degree in "Mathematics for Teaching" that enables young teachers to learn advanced math from professors at the university while also learning how to cope with the daily challenges in the classroom.

In such a rapidly changing world, ongoing professional development needs to be an integral part of every teacher's job beyond the occasional in-service day. Recent research indicates that at least 60 to 80 hours of intensive participation in development programs may be required to bring significant changes in teaching practice. But in 2003, less than a third of math and science teachers in secondary schools attended professional development programs for 33 hours or more over the course of the year.

VERY COMMITTED SCIENTISTS

In math and science education, there are additional challenges resulting from the extra schooling required to teach these subjects adequately and the pay scales of competing alternatives in industry. "If you're coming out of UC Berkeley, you can go be a teacher for $27,000 a year or an entry-level engineer at XYZ Company for $90,000. What would *you* do?" asks Meg Whitman. With the current salary structure, those with bachelor's or master's degrees in science have to be *very* committed to teaching indeed.

Some elementary school teachers may have taken only one introductory course in math or science while earning their teaching credentials. "Many teachers are very fearful of science and math," says Sally Ride, "so they actually teach in a way that discourages kids from asking questions." But learning how to ask questions and test hypotheses makes these subjects interesting and is crucial in learning how to think like a scientist. In middle school and high school, the proportion of science teachers who have advanced degrees in physics, chemistry, and biology is much lower than it should be. In the fifth through eighth grades, most math or science teachers do not have degrees or certificates in those subjects. Yet eight out of ten phys-ed teachers have specialized degrees.

In 2004, mathematician and hedge-fund manager Jim Simons launched a program called Math for America to recruit, train, and retain outstanding teachers for secondary schools by providing fellowships to college graduates and mid-career professionals. The program—which offers full-tuition scholarships and annual stipends—includes a year spent earning a graduate degree in education, and then four years teaching in public schools. MfA also provides Master Teacher Fellowships that reward exceptional teachers with stipends and opportunities for professional development and collaboration with other teachers. Simons founded the program in hopes that he could get the federal government to replicate it on a national level. The 2007 America COMPETES Act includes fellowships modeled after the MfA approach. Let's hope the government backs it up with the funding to get the job done.

It will take time to achieve the level of math and science competence that we need in our schools. Mutually beneficial collaborations between academia and industry could encourage scientists, mathematicians, and engineers to teach part time, consult on curriculum development, or tutor teachers on a volunteer basis. Engineers and scientists who have retired or have lost their jobs to offshoring could also be engaged as a potential source of expertise for schools by providing them with additional training to bring them into the classroom.

Teaching math and science skills presents a special challenge because students need to understand each level before moving on to the next. In an increasingly mobile society without consistent educational standards, it's too easy for students to miss a step along the way. Students can potentially skip over important subjects completely or end up reviewing material over and over again. This could be avoided with a national consensus on broad guidelines for such milestones as when fractions and decimals should be taught, whether physics should be learned first as the basis for lessons in chemistry and biology, and what minimum levels of math and science education are required for graduation. These guidelines could be generated by fruitful collaborations between the U.S. Department of Education, state officials, and agencies like the NSF and the National Academies. "It's possible for a family to move from one state to another and have their kids never be taught decimals. That's just ridiculous," says Sally Ride. Agreeing on a shared set of federal milestones would not be interfering with states' power to select a curriculum—it would just be ensuring that kids throughout the country are getting the same basic level of education.

The only way to effect lasting change in education is by having innovative leadership on school boards and in principals' offices. We need these positions filled by people who are science-literate and who understand the overall requirements of a twenty-first-century education and the particular needs of those who are cultivating the next generation of innovators. A nonprofit group called Scientists and Engineers for America was formed in 2007 to "renew respect for evidence-based debate and decision-making in politics and at all levels of government." One of its goals is to encourage scientists and engineers to run for positions on local school boards. "Creationists have had some success in influencing the direction of education," says Daniel Goroff. "There is no reason why professionals who know something about math and science shouldn't be involved in really serious ways. Our future depends on it."

REFLECTING INNOVATION'S CORE VALUES

It's a challenge for even the best teachers to keep today's kids engaged for more than five minutes. Our curricula and teaching styles need updating, and we can look to the core values of innovation to provide guidance.

The learning process should start at a very early age by encouraging questioning and openness. The fundamentals of reading, math, and history can too easily turn into unrelated bits of information that are memorized, only to be forgotten. Emphasizing the need to ask questions and frame problems correctly requires smaller class sizes and more individualized teaching styles. To cultivate the innovative potential in our students, we need to find ways of rewarding imagination, flexibility, and good judgment, rather than just giving them points for executing sets of rules.

When Steve Scharf, a teacher and administrator in Michigan for 30 years, became principal of a public high school in 1986, less than one in four of the kids enrolled there went on to college. With the support of an open-minded superintendent of schools, Scharf set out to make some changes. First, he reduced the average class size and cut the traditional six-period day to four periods. Teachers took advantage of the longer class times by employing a wide range of methods—from lectures, to group work, to multimedia presentations, to discussion sections—to maintain interest. "Kids learn in different ways at different times," Scharf observes. "If we vary how we teach, our chances of getting through to each student are highly increased." After Scharf put these changes into effect, the number of students who continued their education after high school rose from 24 to 64 percent.

Assigning kids to different tracks early in their education can disadvantage some students, but we also have to be realistic and acknowledge that college will not be the right choice for everyone. Pushing some kids toward goals they are unlikely to achieve creates even more disenchantment with education. We need to provide them with viable alternatives to life on the streets by providing the necessary vocational skills to excel in the twenty-first-century workforce. I took shop in high school at the urging of my father, and I remember the teacher teasing me because I was the only girl in the class; today, I might not even have the option, because many vocational programs have been cut.

Improvements in math and science education should not be made by sacrificing other subjects. Learning about literature, history, and the arts encourages curiosity, creativity, collaboration, and communication, all of which are essential skills for potential innovators. "If I had to teach creative problem solving, would I go to mathematics, physics, or engineering? No," says scientist John Seely Brown. "I would go to history and art for lessons in moral development. Those are the domains that build the aesthetics and sensibilities for the kind of thinking we need."

To cultivate next-generation innovators, the most important skill we need to teach our children is how to learn. "With students focused on getting into the right middle school, because they have to get into the right high school, because they have to get into the right college," says entrepreneur Marc Andreessen, "it's a miracle that public education does not beat the curiosity right out of our kids."

One of the countries pushing the hardest to become a nation of innovators is Singapore. After a period of national obsession with excelling on standardized tests, students were able to score very well in science, technology, engineering, and math—but something was missing. The students weren't thinking creatively. "If you go to Singapore now, you discover that the game has completely changed. Now the mantra is 'teach less, learn more,'" says Seely Brown, who chairs a committee for the ministry of education there. Now the country is implementing what's called the *full inquiry method*, with teachers emphasizing questioning among small groups of students. "I've watched groups of seventh graders doing Newtonian mechanics, all trying to get a gut understanding of what Newton's laws actually mean. Then they have to explain their understanding to other kids in the class. It's just awesome," he says.

MAKING MATH AND SCIENCE FUN

In 2001, Sally Ride formed a company called Sally Ride Science (SRS) to tap into kids' natural curiosity by offering exciting educational materials and programs that would sustain their interest through middle school, imparting the message that science is fun. "We don't try to make our classroom materials be comprehensive treatises on the subject, but rather things that are entertaining and cool while really capturing kids' interest," she says. Kids leave SRS summer camps energized, enthused, and determined to enroll in science classes at school. Their parents also end up learning something essential: that their children could have a future in science.

Bringing students into a working lab is one of the best ways to get them excited about science. A former Genentech researcher named George Cachianes now teaches biotech courses at Lincoln High in San Francisco. Each class is divided into teams of five students who purify proteins and create their own DNA sequences, making the abstract subject of genetics come to life. One of Cachianes's high school teams entered a contest at MIT to compete against 57 teams from universities around the world, and was one of the six finalists. "Our kids can shatter limits if we take a risk and give them a chance to try," he told the *New York Times*.

Turning math and science into the equivalent of team sports is another way of sparking kids' interest. In 1989, one of America's most prolific inventors, Dean Kamen (father of the Segway human transporter, a mobile dialysis system, and the all-terrain wheelchair) founded an organization called FIRST, which sponsors robot-building competitions for high school students and volunteers. The size of the competitions has grown from less than 30 teams to more than 1,300 over the years, and Kamen's group has now added a "Lego League" to involve younger children. "The robot competition has taken kids in the inner cities and shown them that they have a better chance of being able to buy a house for their mother some day by becoming an engineer than by ending up in the NBA," says entrepreneur Audrey MacLean.

We need more programs like this that leverage kids' innate curiosity and demonstrate the benefits of achievement in math, science, and engineering. In an age in which more and more science is being done remotely, even kids in far-flung places can share the excitement—and the equipment. "Probably 5 to 10 percent of the time on the supercomputers at the National Center of Atmospheric Research is taken up by high school students looking at climate models," says John Seely Brown.

The word *engineering* does not typically show up in curricula until college. But exposing kids to real-world engineering problems can motivate them to learn about math or science by making it less theoretical. We need to bring engineering into the classroom and the playground by giving kids the thrill of building things.

Generations of innovators grew up tinkering with engines and electronics. "I know a lot of people who built computers from kits, and every one of them turned into an entrepreneur in Silicon Valley," says entrepreneur Martin Eberhard. But as our technologies have grown more complex, it has become harder and harder to "look under the hood." Danny Hillis of Applied Minds observes, "You can't take the current generation of computers apart. If you try, there's just a little chip there, and you can't look inside it." Kids who are already interested in tinkering and do-it-yourself tech can find all sorts of products, useful information, and communities of fellow tinkerers online—but they need to know where to look. The Internet has introduced a new kind of virtual tinkering in the form of open-source code, remixing music, and making mash-ups of media. But these things do not replace the hands-on experimentation that might inspire a future scientist or civil engineer.

Our kids have lost much of their ability to explore and experiment in the real world. "Today's kids are experiencing phenomenal overprotection. Every parent I know is mesmerized about whether their kids are safe, and they won't let kids explore outside of the house," says John Seely Brown. Kids' activities and families' lives are so tightly scheduled that nothing has been left to chance.

There are still ways for children to experiment and get their hands dirty in programs like FIRST's robotics contests. But home chemistry and amateur rocketry are now being threatened by legislation like the Federal Hazardous Substances Act and the Homeland Security Act. Most of the chemicals that were once staples of home chemistry sets are now illegal to sell to children. Even in science classrooms, fears about safety and liability are limiting hands-on experimentation. We should not replace time in a chemistry lab with passively watching videos, which turns science into a spectator sport.

EDUCATIONAL R&D

There are now laws in nearly 40 states that allow the establishment of so-called charter schools—publicly funded institutions that are exempt from some of the rules and regulations that apply within the mainstream public school system. The promise of charter schools is that they will introduce the element of choice and competition into the process of selecting the best school for your child. These schools should also be testing grounds for educational innovations that can flow outward to the public schools once they are proven effective. In practice, however, this hasn't always been the case. "A lot of the folks who advocated charter schools thought that they would be an effective laboratory for new ideas," says Brian Gill, a senior social scientist at Mathematica Policy Research, Inc. "But there's been very little evidence thus far that any new ideas in the charter schools have been disseminated very well to public schools, if at all." We need better mechanisms to share information and learn from the successes and failures in all of our schools.

We should also be experimenting more with the role that supplemental education can play in creating the next generation of innovators. There is a thriving industry now that is focused on getting students into top-tier high schools and colleges by offering coaching and tutoring for standardized tests. What if we expanded our notion of supplemental education to include programs that boosted our kids' imaginations and their confidence to explore new subjects?

The good news is that technology is finally making a difference in the classroom. E-mail and Web sites have increased communication among students, teachers, parents, and school administrators. The Internet has become a powerful research tool for students. The next step is to determine how computers can be used to enhance learning through individualized lesson plans, online access to experts and other students, and immersive educational environments. For just a few thousand dollars, we can now build virtual worlds that would have cost millions a few years ago. "I got wrapped up into a protein in a 3-D game a few months ago," says John Seely Brown. "Now I know why protein folding is so complicated. Before that, I had no visceral sense of what a protein was." Computation and visualization can bring dry science lessons alive, and even restore a sense of awe about the ways the universe works.

NO CHILD LEFT BEHIND?

The goal of the No Child Left Behind Act (NCLB), passed in 2001, was to improve the accountability and performance of primary and secondary schools throughout the country. NCLB is based on the notion that all kids ought to be able to achieve proficiency in reading and math, as measured by standardized tests. The evidence that these tests provide an accurate gauge of learning, however, is very mixed. And they may not even be a very effective way to measure school performance, because kids come into the system with widely varying levels of prior achievement, preparation, and family support. They also don't measure the extent to which schools succeed in reducing dropouts.

Federal law requires each state to set its own standards for proficiency, and schools are graded on the proportion of kids who have reached that level. But because there are no national standards, expectations for kids' performance varies from state to state. If a school misses the mark for "adequate yearly progress," it gets a warning. If it misses a second time, the school gets tagged with "identify for improvement" and has to offer its students the opportunity to transfer to another school. But in the real world, very few students are able or willing to make a transfer. "It's a kind of public school choice provision that is getting almost no participation," says Brian Gill. "Nationally, the best evidence is that about 1 percent of the kids who are in these schools are actually taking advantage of that option."

If a school misses its benchmarks for a third year in a row, its low-income students must be offered "supplemental educational services." A portion of the federal funds that would have gone to the school is redirected to tutoring services offered by a range of public and private providers. "The participation rates aren't terribly high there either—on the order of 15 to 20 percent," says Gill. Even so, those percentages reflect a large number of students; thus, NCLB has created an enormous private market in after-school tutoring by taking already-scarce federal dollars out of the public schools.

Beyond the third year, much more aggressive interventions are introduced that can include replacing the school's staff and administration, converting it to a charter school, or bringing in private management. And the states have to ratchet up their standards each year until 2014, when 100 percent of the kids are supposed to be proficient. A larger and larger number of schools are going to fall short and become subject to these interventions. Realistically speaking, many states may not have the resources to institute turnaround plans for large numbers of schools.

What is not at all clear is whether NCLB is actually helping to prepare our students for the future. There is growing evidence that other subjects and enrichment activities are being sacrificed to focus on the subjects for which schools are held accountable, as measured by standardized tests. "Teaching to a test can affect not only the subject that's being tested, but those that are not," Sally Ride observes. "So much focus is put on the tested areas that there is no time left in the school day for other important subjects." The opportunity to introduce our children to art, music, drama, vocational skills, and even science is being compromised, as teachers are driven to maximize test results. A recent study of Bay Area elementary school teachers found that 80 percent of them spend less than an hour each week teaching science—and that 16 percent do not teach it at all.

At least education is now recognized as a critical national priority. "For all of its flaws, No Child Left Behind is the most ambitious federal intervention into K-12 schooling in American history. I think that is unambiguous," says Gill, acknowledging that it is "a blunt instrument." But NCLB is not merely blunt—it is the wrong instrument. Instead of setting national guidelines and encouraging schools to use testing data as valuable guidance for frank self-assessment, NCLB ends up encouraging behaviors that actually impair the development of innovative minds. Trying to prepare every student for a four-year college education has forced schools to eliminate vocational and other programs. We are no longer giving kids the options that are particularly important for the less-advantaged children that NCLB was intended to help.

In an era when we talk so much about Web site personalization, we are not giving our children the opportunity to develop as individuals. We need students who are solidly grounded in the fundamentals, but also generations of innovators who discovered their passion by being exposed to a broad range of human creativity and knowledge in school. We will not lead in the future by producing a nation of robots.

PREPARED MINDS

The requirements for change at the college level are not all that different from those for K-12. In 2006, the U.S. Department of Education published an evaluation of postsecondary education called *A Test of True Leadership*. The report highlights the importance of science and technology education, identifies the need to provide access to a broader range of students, and stresses the necessity of teaching students the skills that they will need to enter the workplace. The report also stresses the need for "accountability" and "efficiency" in higher education. In practice, however, these words are often used to make the kinds of changes in the classroom that leave no room for innovation.

Neuroscientist Jamshed Bharucha took a hard look at test-centric pedagogical methods in the *Chronicle of Higher Education* and came to the conclusion that an emphasis on rote drills and memorization will not provide the answers we need. "The more varied the learning context, the more likely it is that the learning will manifest itself in one's thinking in the future—which is the object of education," he wrote in 2008. "We learn more effectively when we generate the material to be learned than when we passively receive it." At its best, our system promotes learning by giving students more choices among an array of diverse teaching and testing styles. Let's not trade off the ability to train our students to think broadly, frame questions, and collaborate for the sake of coming up with easy ways to benchmark their achievements.

We need to make sure that our educational programs meet the rapidly changing demands of the job market. Most interdisciplinary programs that start at the graduate level at universities should also be extended to undergraduates. The twenty-first-century workplace requires more people who can translate knowledge between disciplines. "We need engineers who know about nanomaterials and biology, and who understand how materials behave in the environment as well as having fundamental skills in chemistry and IT," says VC John Doerr. There's an increasing need for professionals in other fields to understand not only programming, but also problem solving based on computational thinking.

Learning how to solve problems efficiently is at the heart of traditional science education, but students also need to learn how to frame questions, not just answer them. "The educational process focuses too much on solving existing problems, and does not focus enough on giving students the tools to define important problems themselves," says scientist Peter Schultz. This kind of learning is best taught in small groups with lots of discussion, and it requires teachers to act as facilitators as well as lecturers.

To foster innovation, we need to supplement traditional courses in science and engineering with training in leadership. In the medical technology area, Stanford offers a program called Biodesign, which adds a layer of what the university calls "innovation education" to the traditional curriculum, focusing on identifying and screening needs and on multidisciplinary invention and implementation. After six years, the program has sparked eight venture-backed companies and four FDA-approved technologies.

One of the strengths of our educational system is the diversity of its postsecondary institutions, ranging from big research universities to community colleges. But as the size of the endowments of private colleges has grown, there is a widening gap between private and public education. We must ensure that public institutions are adequately funded and continue to encourage charitable contributions to all educational institutions. Many of the private universities are starting to leverage their large endowments to benefit the Ecosystem by increasing their financial aid programs. "We were quite successful in making it so that any qualified student below the median income in the United States could come to Princeton for free," says Jeremiah Ostriker, who was provost of the university from 1995 to 2001.

Academic grants based on merit became unpopular in the 1960s, when it was unfashionable to insist that some students are inherently more gifted than others. "I am appalled that there are fewer and fewer merit scholarships in the United States," says Ostriker. "I would institute federal merit scholarships at universities so that the top 1 percent of students in every congressional district would be eligible." Reviving merit scholarships not only would provide more opportunities for all students with the most potential, but would send an important message to underprivileged kids that improved academic performance is worthy of payback.

Strengthening our community colleges could relieve four-year colleges from having to do as much remedial education as they do, and also provide opportunities for vocational training and for older students to learn new skills. Not every high school graduate can realistically aim to enroll in an intensive four-year program. "I think we've underfunded our community colleges," says Stanford president John Hennessy. "While the UC system is the jewel of California's public higher education system, it's only part of it, and the bulk of the burden is going to have to be carried by the state universities and community colleges." These schools also need to ensure that they have the capabilities to train people for rewarding jobs in the information economy, not just entry-level positions that are being increasingly offshored.

We need nurturing educational environments that encourage the core values of innovation, enabling college students to learn *how* to learn while figuring out what they want to pursue in life. Undergraduates may need extra help, especially in science and engineering, where their high school educations have often been barely adequate. "When they show up as freshmen, start nurturing right there," says Autodesk chairman Carol Bartz. "Especially the young women. Don't drum them out. Nurture them."

One of the ways we can encourage students to study science, technology, engineering, and math is by making sure that they are aware of the burgeoning job opportunities in these areas. The U.S. Bureau of Labor Statistics predicts that the science and engineering workforce will grow at nearly double the rate of other occupations through 2014. Even for those who decide that they don't want a career in technology or research, a solid education in science and math lays the groundwork for many other opportunities, including those in business. "The best entrepreneurs are those who have a background in science, engineering, or medicine, not a business background," says SRI's Curtis Carlson. "You want to add the business on top of the science and engineering, not the other way around."

Despite the widespread perception that the job market for computer scientists declined after the collapse of the dot-com bubble, there are more software jobs available in the United States today than at the height of the boom. But the number of graduates each year with the necessary skills is dropping. "Looking at the twenty-first-century workforce, we are bordering on a crisis," says Telle Whitney, president of the Anita Borg Institute, founded in 1997 to "increase the impact of women on all aspects of technology, and increase the positive impact of technology on the world's women." In 1987, women accounted for nearly 40 percent of those graduating with computing degrees, but that number has plummeted to 28 percent. One of the reasons why the ABI has such strong industry support—from companies like Microsoft and Sun—is that technology businesses recognize that educating and hiring more women is one of the most promising ways to stave off a crisis.

THE IMPORTANCE OF CULTURAL CONTEXT

Education does not begin and end in the classroom. Young people's attitudes are profoundly influenced by the culture at large, and there, too, forces working against the development of future generations of innovators are in play.

The Internet has had many positive impacts on our lives, but the availability of up-to-the-minute information at our fingertips has contributed to a focus on instant gratification—not only in the business world, but in all areas of life. Training kids to think deeply about issues has been replaced by Googling for an easy answer. Young people who have grown up in the Internet era have become used to having things right away, which is not how the world works. "A lot of my peers at business school have gone off to work at great companies, but almost all of them are looking for a new job after only a year out," says Abby Josephs, who just received a joint master's in business and public health from UC Berkeley. "They have the idea that the world is going to always be exciting. Then they get slotted into a project management role and find that their actual universe can be pretty boring and disappointing." The postbubble generation doesn't want to work its way to the top—it just wants to *be* there. The virtue of patience has been nearly forgotten.

The proliferation of choices in personal life has also contributed to a lack of focus among young people. "Our parents grew up in a world where they had to make three decisions by their twenty-fifth birthday—whom they were going to marry, where they were going to live, and what they were going to do professionally, " observes investor Roger McNamee. "They didn't have a lot of choices. Now we have a million choices, but we're entirely at the mercy of our own judgment and skills." Instilling in our kids both trust in themselves and the judgment to know who else to trust is critical. With so many options, it's important for them to have tenacity and not give up too quickly, while also being able to cope with failure by using it to learn and adapt. They need to be taught that they personally can make a difference.

One of the main cultural messages that has been lost to young people in recent years is that scientists and engineers tackle problems that are of crucial relevance to our lives. Instead of being hailed as heroes, as they were during the post-Sputnik era, scientists are often portrayed as socially awkward geeks. "My peers on the whole consider science and math as subjects for the ultra-smart and nerdy, while excelling in the humanities is normal," says my son David. "The marketing for this anti-science and math sentiment is like a virus, and not an easy one to kill."

We live in a celebrity culture, where appearance, money, and scandals prevail. "There's a ubiquity to media today that is pervasive, so kids are seeing a lot more of it than they ever did before," says Disney's Bob Iger. You don't have to walk on the moon to be a hero of science; when heart transplants were new, Iger points out, the first surgeon to successfully perform one, Dr. Christiaan Barnard, appeared on the cover of *Time* magazine. "As a society, we need to figure out again how to portray science as a noble vocation," says chemistry professor Richard Zare.

The next frontiers of science are not in space, but right here on Earth. Fighting climate change, battling cancer and other diseases, and finding new forms of energy to replace oil are all noble missions. To motivate the next generation of innovators, we need a new breed of cultural heroes.

REACHING OUT

Teachers and business leaders should not underestimate the role that mentoring can play in inspiring and nurturing kids and young adults. Many great careers were launched when someone took the time to reach out and recognize the talent of a student or a young employee. "I discovered computer science in college," says Telle Whitney of the Anita Borg Institute. "A teacher noticed me and introduced me to somebody who was starting the program at Cal Tech. It's that touch that makes a difference."

Today, Esther Sternberg is well recognized for her discoveries in the effects of the brain's stress response on health. But when she began her research in the 1980s, her work was not well accepted. "It came very close to being killed a number of times. I had the good fortune to have either sought out or accidentally met people who were supportive," she says. "They weren't the majority, but they were enough. It just takes one or two." For every Sternberg, there must be hundreds of young scientists who came up against similar obstacles and didn't get the help they needed to push through them. The science community needs to get more involved in actively mentoring young minds. An opportunity to visit a working lab or a summer internship at an innovative company can make a big difference in a high school student's life.

Obviously, the most important mentors a child can have are his or her own parents. We should encourage our kids to ask questions by taking the time to sit and listen to them. We need to give them the time and space to explore the world, both online and off. We must demonstrate our love and trust so that they feel confident about trying new things, even if they occasionally fail and have to pick themselves back up again. We need to show them the joys of creating, not just the joys of consuming, and to teach them that the pleasure of learning is more important than being anxious about getting a good grade. Community and nonprofit organizations that step in where parents can't, providing additional nurturing, education, and inspiration for less advantaged kids, deserve our support.

Parents send messages to their kids without even realizing it. One mother introduced her 11-year-old daughter to Sally Ride at a science fair. She told Ride how proud she was of her daughter for being the star of her math class, but she went on to say, "I don't know where she gets it, because I was never any good in math, and I don't know any women who are." Ride could see the little girl pull inside herself as she absorbed the subliminal message that her interest in math was not normal. At that age, there is nothing more important than feeling normal.

When it comes to communicating the message that science and innovation are crucial for our future, our culture is even more broken than our schools. We need to recognize that we will not be able to stay this shortsighted and win. We're living our lives like day traders, when we need to be making long-term investments in our nation's future. Our children and grand-children are worth it.

A CALL
TO ACTION

I have never been an alarmist, but in the course of writing this book, I have become more and more concerned about the state of our future. My initial motivation was prompted by the nearsightedness that had taken over my part of the world, in Silicon Valley and on Wall Street. But as I did my research and talked to other business and scientific leaders, I realized that our Innovation Ecosystem has become even more eroded and unstable than I could have imagined.

The curiosity and openness that have defined the American character since the founding of this country have been replaced by fear and apathy. The patience to cultivate potentially great things for the future has been trumped by a mania for instant gratification. The national trust necessary to build alliances with the rest of the world is gone, as is our willingness to take the risks that are required to make significant breakthroughs. The complex web of interrelationships among science, technology, innovation, and economic growth has been either taken for granted by our leaders or utterly forgotten. Our planning horizons are focused purely on making things better for today, this quarter, or this year, with hardly any thought for the fate of future generations. The generation of innovators growing up in America today will be forced to seek success *in spite of* our educational system and a culture that demeans and dismisses

231

science as either a nerdy preoccupation or an agenda-laden collection of mere "theories."

The threats to our future are becoming more apparent every day. Since I started writing this book, our economy has experienced a precipitous downturn, the price of crude oil has doubled, and our dependence on foreign sources of energy has only increased. The war in Iraq continues at great cost—in lives and dollars, in our national unity, and in our standing in the world. The subprime mortgage crisis (an unintended consequence of actions taken to stabilize our economy as far back as 2001) was created by the same kind of greed, short-term thinking, and disregard for consequences that fostered the Internet bubble. Did we learn nothing from the dot-com bust?

But it's not too late to take the actions necessary to save our future, and there are already glimmerings of hope on the horizon. Globalization—which was initially greeted by fear and distrust—has opened up huge new markets for American businesses. This hasn't helped the workers whose jobs have been shipped overseas, but it's better than the alternative, which is no business growth at all. Awareness of some of the problems that we face as a nation has grown, but we now need to commit ourselves to addressing them. This year will bring a welcome change in our nation's leadership. More people are interested in the electoral process and are voting than in the past. Hopefully their votes will be informed by an understanding of the challenges we face. We need not just a new administration in the White House, but a new kind of national leadership.

The world is poised for a huge leap in the rate of innovation as a result of the enhanced sharing of information and the collaborative possibilities opened up by the Internet. We need to be leading actors in this enormous global transformation, rather than merely spectators.

The challenges that we face are wide-ranging and deeply embedded in our culture. Repositioning ourselves to thrive in the new global economy will take time. Some of the transitions will not be easy, but I have faith that with courage, commitment, and the boldness that has always distinguished the most successful innovators and entrepreneurs, we can execute this major change in course together as a nation.

The business community must be willing to reembrace intelligent risk taking while placing more value on potential growth. Corporate leaders can do what's right for their shareholders while considering what's right for society as a whole. Companies are already becoming very creative in learning how to "work green." Business leaders, policy makers, and educators will need to work together to find economically viable ways to increase employment opportunities in the United States while ensuring a steady supply of innovative talent—from home and abroad—to take on these jobs. If we don't take a hard look at the growing gaps between the rich and the poor, we will risk ending up in an America with no middle class at all.

In my roles as a business leader over the past several decades, I learned how important it is to be fiscally responsible; but I also learned that if an important initiative is funded below critical mass, nothing ever happens. We must increase our investments in education and research. To revitalize our Innovation Ecosystem will require more than just new leaders at the federal level. We also need to cultivate the leadership qualities in our own lives to reclaim America's role in the future. As parents, mentors, or media figures, we need to think very carefully about the messages we send to the next generation.

Innovation is driven by necessity, and the necessity of taking decisive action is what we're facing now as a nation and as citizens of the world. As we tackle these challenges together, we must remember to consider the indispensable roles that all three communities of the Ecosystem will play in securing a future in which our children can thrive. We must tap the boldness of our national heritage to inspire us to make changes at both disruptive and incremental levels, while remembering that failure can be just another step toward success if you're determined to honestly self-assess and learn from every experience.

My son, David, starts college this year. I never question his capacity to make the best of whatever comes his way, but I worry about the state of our society as he embarks on his path to adulthood. We have created many of the problems that our children will inherit, and we owe them at least the first steps toward solutions, along with the message that courage, confidence, and patience will be required to reach the goal of a sustainable world. My hope for those of David's generation—and for their children and grandchildren—is that they will map their own new pathways to success by asking the right questions, taking calculated risks, opening their hearts and minds to the world around them, and trusting just enough in themselves and others to make the long journey together.

ACKNOWLEDGMENTS

Like a typical entrepreneur, I embarked upon this journey not knowing what lay ahead. Creating a book is very different from leading a company, but they have something in common. While many people contributed their input and their ideas, ultimately I must take responsibility for the synthesis and for any errors or omissions. This book represents my perspectives, not those of the companies I am affiliated with.

There are so many people who expanded my outlook as I wrote this book. I benefited from the insight and experience of the diverse set of accomplished people that I interviewed, listed on the following pages. I'm thankful to each one of them for sharing his or her time and views. To all the friends and colleagues with whom I had informal discussions over coffee, at board meetings, and while walking "the Dish," thank you for listening, reading drafts, making introductions, and sparking new ideas. Thanks in particular to Mike Afergan, Denise Amantea, George Anders, Geoff Baehr, Alan Braverman, Betsy Corcoran, Tim Danford, Lara Druyan, Andrea Goldsmith, Amal Johnson, Roberta Katz, Doug Klein, Ellen Levy, Judy O'Brien, Liz Perle, Kamini Ramani, Carol Realini, Karen Rossetto, Naomi Seligman, Estee Solomon Gray, and Teddy Zmrhal. Marnin Kligfeld, my brother-in-law, deserves special gratitude for his ongoing support and insightful comments at all stages of the manuscript. I also want to thank all of the people who worked with me over the years as colleagues or employees. I learned something valuable about innovation from each one of you.

I would like to thank my network of researchers, each of whom made important contributions: Karen Dunn-Haley, Cynthia Eastman, Karen Hembourgh, Abby Josephs, David Sanford, and Susan Stucky. Reports and statistics published by the National Science Foundation and the National Academies also helped inform this book. The NSF's *Science and Engineering Indicators* and the National Academies' *Rising Above the Gathering Storm* and *Is America Falling Off the Flat Earth?* were all especially helpful.

Without Mary Glenn and the staff at McGraw-Hill, this book would not exist. My agent, Laura Yorke, has been ready with support and advice ever since our first phone conversation, when she helped me decide what path to take to best communicate my message.

I was fortunate enough to convince Steve Silberman, an incredibly talented writer for *Wired* magazine and other publications, to act as my writing coach and editor. Steve's commentary, questions, and advice helped me to find my own written voice and then amplified it with his editing.

Susan Kare, the creative artist who brought us the original Macintosh icons, did the illustrations. Thank you, Susan, for applying your magic to the key message of each chapter.

My assistant and dear friend Stevie Jagutis helps me juggle my obligations and keep track of my life. Thank you, Stevie, for everything you do, and also for helping with research and reviewing drafts.

I want to thank my former husband, Bill Carrico. As my first mentor, he recognized abilities in me that I didn't see in myself when he promoted me to my first management position. Many of the lessons I learned about innovation I learned with Bill as we created our companies.

For the past several years, I have been questioning many of my own assumptions in my own personal journey of innovation and change. Thanks to Gary Wynbrandt for his support and for helping me to connect the dots.

My sisters have always been there for me in ways that only sisters can be, and the process of writing this book was no exception. They both provided input, reviewed drafts, and listened to me when I didn't think the writing would ever be done. Several of the companies that I helped create were based on research pioneered by Deborah; to me, she represents the kind of people we need in order to rebuild the foundation of the Ecosystem. Margo is not only a doctor, but also a caring big sister who is always available to me, no matter what else is going on in her day. Through the years, whenever I have had to do something difficult, she has said, "I am in your pocket." This past year, she has lived in my pocket.

I thank my parents for exposing me to the beauty of science and instilling in me a love of learning, the willingness to try something new, and the drive and discipline to push harder when things get tough.

And finally, to my son, David, thank you for bringing joy and inspiration into my life every day.

LIST OF INTERVIEWEES

Miley Ainsworth, director of IT innovation, FedEx Corporation

Marc Andreessen, chairman and cofounder, Ning

Norman (Norm) Augustine, retired chairman and CEO, Lockheed Martin Corporation

Paul Baran, Internet pioneer

Carol Bartz, executive chairman, Autodesk

Forest Baskett, general partner, New Enterprise Associates

Eric Benhamou, CEO, Benhamou Global Ventures

Joel Birnbaum, retired senior vice president for R&D, Hewlett-Packard

John Seely Brown, former chief scientist, Xerox

Curtis R. Carlson, CEO, SRI International

Bill Carrico, entrepreneur

Rob Carter, executive vice president and CIO, FedEx Corporation

Ed Catmull, president, Walt Disney and Pixar Animation Studios

Vint Cerf, vice president and chief Internet evangelist, Google

John Chambers, chairman and CEO, Cisco Systems

Mark Chandler, senior vice president and general counsel, Cisco Systems

Anand Chandrasekher, senior vice president, Intel Corporation

David Clark, senior research scientist, MIT

Sam Colella, managing director, Versant Ventures

Kevin Compton, venture capitalist, Kleiner Perkins Caufield & Byers

Scott Cook, chairman of the executive committee, Intuit

Bill Coughran, senior vice president, engineering, Google

John Cronin, managing director and chairman, ipCapital Group

David Culler, professor of computer science, UC Berkeley

Peter Currie, president, Currie Capital

Carol Dahl, director, Global Health Discovery; chief of staff, Global Health Program, Bill & Melinda Gates Foundation

Yogen Dalal, managing director, Mayfield Fund

John Doerr, partner, Kleiner Perkins Caufield & Byers

Martin Eberhard, entrepreneur

Hossein Eslambolchi, chairman, Divvio

Deborah Estrin, professor, computer science, UCLA; director, Center for Embedded Networked Sensing (CENS)

Nathan Estruth, general manager, FutureWorks, Procter & Gamble

Brian Gill, senior social scientist, Mathematica Policy Research

Steven Goldby, executive chairman, Symyx Technologies

Daniel Goroff, professor, mathematics and economics, Harvey Mudd College

Andy Grove, former CEO, Intel Corporation

Gary Guthart, president and COO, Intuitive Surgical

Peter Hart, president, Ricoh Innovations; group senior vice president, Ricoh Company

Eric Haseltine, managing partner, Haseltine Partners

Reed Hastings, CEO, Netflix

Jeff Hawkins, cofounder, Numenta

John Hennessy, president, Stanford University

Danny Hillis, cochairman, Applied Minds

Reid Hoffman, chairman, LinkedIn

Krisztina Holly, vice provost for innovation and executive director, USC Stevens Institute for Innovation at the University of Southern California

Joe Huber, vice president, sales, Arch Rock

Bob Iger, CEO, The Walt Disney Company

Laura Ipsen, senior vice president, global policy & government affairs, Cisco Systems

Van Jacobson, research fellow, PARC

Ryan Jagutis, teacher, Chicago Public Schools

Abby Josephs, program manager, Stanford Hospital and Clinics

Mark Josephs, emergency department physician director, Exeter Hospital

Tom Kalil, special assistant to the chancellor for science & technology, UC Berkeley

Alan Kay, president, Viewpoints Research Institute

David Kelley, professor of mechanical engineering, Stanford University

Joe Kennedy, CEO, Omneon

David Kessler, former commissioner of the U.S. FDA

Joel Klein, chancellor, New York City Department of Education

E. Floyd Kvamme, partner emeritus, Kleiner Perkins Caufield & Byers

Larry Lasky, venture partner, U.S. Venture Partners

Ellen Levy, managing director, Silicon Valley Connect

David Liddle, partner, U.S. Venture Partners

Robert Lucky, former executive director, Bell Labs

Audrey MacLean, entrepreneur and mentor capitalist

John Markoff, senior writer, *New York Times*

Martha Marsh, president and CEO, Stanford Hospital & Clinics

Roger McNamee, managing director, Elevation Partners

Scott McNealy, chairman, Sun Microsystems

Bob Metcalfe, general partner, Polaris Venture Partners

Michael Moritz, partner, Sequoia Capital

Elon Musk, CEO, SpaceX

Dick O'Neill, director, The Highlands Forum

June Osborn, professor emerita of epidemiology, pediatrics and communicable diseases, University of Michigan

Jeremiah Ostriker, professor of astrophysics,
Princeton University

Kal Patel, executive vice president, emerging business,
Best Buy

Arno Penzias, venture partner, NEA; formerly vice president
and chief scientist, Bell Labs

Jim Plummer, dean, School of Engineering, Stanford University

Frank Quattrone, investment banker

Wes Raffel, general partner, Advanced Technology Ventures

Rick Rashid, senior vice president of research, Microsoft

Sally Ride, CEO, Sally Ride Science

Heidi Roizen, CEO, SkinnySongs

Paul Romer, professor of economics, Stanford University

Jon Rubinstein, executive chairman, Palm

George Scalise, president, Semiconductor Industry Association

Steve Scharf, retired high school principal

Eric Schmidt, chairman and CEO, Google

Peter Schultz, director, Genomics Institute of the Novartis
Research Foundation

Randy Scott, chairman and CEO, Genomic Health

Michael Sheridan, venture capitalist

John Shoch, general partner, Alloy Ventures

Len Shustek, chairman of the board of trustees, Computer
History Museum

Fredrick W. (Fred) Smith, chairman and CEO, FedEx
Corporation

Lonnie Smith, chairman and CEO, Intuitive Surgical

Robert Spinrad, former director, Xerox PARC

Esther Sternberg, chief, Section on Neuroendocrine Immunology and Behavior, National Institute of Mental Health

David Tennenhouse, partner, New Venture Partners

Malay Thaker, director of customer solutions, Arch Rock

Mary Ann Thode, president, Kaiser Foundation Health Plan and Hospitals, Northern California Region

Henry Tirri, vice president and head of NRC systems research, Nokia

Charles Vest, president, National Academy of Engineering; president emeritus of MIT

Mike Volpi, CEO, Joost

Lezlee Westine, CEO, TechNet

Meg Whitman, former president and CEO, eBay

Telle Whitney, CEO, Anita Borg Institute for Women and Technology

Susan F. Wood, research professor, George Washington University School of Public Health and Health Services

Paul Yock, professor of bioengineering and medicine, Stanford University

Richard Zare, professor of chemistry, Stanford University

INDEX

ABOUT THE AUTHOR

Judy Estrin (Menlo Park, CA) is CEO of JLABS, LLC, formerly known as Packet Design Management Company. Prior to cofounding Packet Design in May 2000, Estrin was chief technology officer for Cisco Systems. Beginning in 1981, Estrin cofounded three other successful technology companies: Bridge Communications, Network Computing Devices, and Precept Software. In 1998 Cisco Systems acquired Precept, and she became Cisco's chief technology officer

Estrin has been named three times to *Fortune* magazine's list of the 50 most powerful women in American business. She sits on the boards of directors of The Walt Disney Company and FedEx Corporation, as well as two private company boards— Packet Design, Inc. and Arch Rock. She also sits on the advisory councils of Stanford's school of Engineering and Stanford's Bio-X initiative, as well as the University of California President's Science and Innovation advisory board. She holds a B.S. degree in math and computer science from UCLA, and an M.S. in electrical engineering from Stanford University.

Join the conversation at www.theinnovationgap.com.